DICKENS'
CHRISTMAS

Compiled by

JOHN HUDSON

SUTTON PUBLISHING

First published in 1997 by
Sutton Publishing Limited · Phoenix Mill
Thrupp · Stroud · Gloucestershire · GL5 2BU

British Library Cataloguing in Publication Data
A catalogue record for this book is available from the British Library

ISBN 0-7509-1502-1

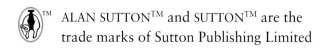 ALAN SUTTON™ and SUTTON™ are the
trade marks of Sutton Publishing Limited

Typeset in 11/15 pt Sabon.
Typesetting and origination by
Sutton Publishing Limited.
Printed in Great Britain by
Ebenezer Baylis, Worcester.

CONTENTS

INTRODUCTION

It is irresistible to credit Charles Dickens with inventing the modern Christmas, or at least the Victorian version to which we still hark back today. Irresistible, but erroneous. What Dickens did, as he did so superbly in other facets of his writing, was scent the spirit of his times, add to it his own special magic and create Christmas confections that were devoured with relish in his day, are being enjoyed 150 years on and will doubtless be so when the twenty-first century that so preoccupies us now has come and gone.

One could make an equally compelling case for other, more prosaic, inventors being the fathers of Christmas as we know it – James Hargreaves of the spinning jenny perhaps, Richard Arkwright of the spinning frame or George Stephenson with his *Rocket*. The fact is that the early giants of the Industrial Revolution helped to usher in times so alien to what had been seen before that by the 1830s everything was in place for the Christmas miracle to take shape and the transformation scene to blossom; this applied not only to Britain but also to the United States, where Washington Irving was as central to the glorification of the season as was Dickens here.

At the heart of this new spirit was a hankering after the 'old Christmas' in the country, before human-kind had become slaves to the burgeoning towns and cities. 'Old Christmases', then as now, were not as glamorous as nostalgia would have us believe, and in many a brutish country hovel of pre-industrial times the anniversary of the nativity would have passed as miserably as any other dreary midwinter day. It is a fact, however, that the well-to-do landowners of the seventeenth century did deck their halls with green boughs and make something of a fuss of each other at that time, and that to salve their consciences they would include their servants and estate workers in the celebrations to the extent of doles of food or clothing and perhaps a trinket for the children.

Come the new age of the early nineteenth century, the country squires did not count for as much as they had done – but the emerging urban middle

classes took greatly to the idea of helping the poor at Christmas time, as well as to the notion of family gatherings around blazing log fires, of entertaining friends and relations and, in particular, of making the season memorable for their children. They were encouraged in this by the generally civilizing effect of comfortably-off people living close to one another, by improving housing conditions, and by the Churches and the temperance movement, which were concerned with the less-than-civilizing effect of town life on those who were far from comfortably-off. In retrospect, we know that the middle-class Victorian psyche was a seething mass of hang-ups and hypocrisies, incongruities and contradictions; but it is not hard to see – and easy to sympathize with – what the doctors and bankers and merchants of Britain were striving for at Christmas in the 1830s and '40s – or to appreciate how, in the next two decades of prosperity, families further down the social ladder took increasingly readily to the idea of midwinter festivities gathered safe around the hearth.

By the 1860s the factory workers whose world revolved around the teeming little streets of London, the North and the Midlands were very different creatures from the wild spirits herded in from the countryside to work the looms three or four generations earlier. They had been schooled in the discipline of regimented work, a life in which you could set your clock by the factory hooter. Their forefathers had rebelled against this oppressive new way of life with great, sprawling binges centred around centuries-old wakes and holidays – booze-befuddled lost weekends which spilled over into the new working week through unofficial days' leave known as 'St Monday's'. By the middle of the nineteenth century this was not the way most working men regulated their lives – though in *A Christmas Carol* we see how even the down-trodden and family-oriented Bob Cratchit allowed himself an extra few minutes' lie-in on Boxing Day morning, in spite of being cursed with an employer who, up until that Christmas, had been the most unreasonable in the world.

In 1834 Christmas Day became one of the few in the year to be recognized as a holiday, and it was 1871 before Parliament came round to the Cratchit way of thinking – a view shared by many at grass-roots level – and formally extended the break to Boxing Day. Other forces were at work, however, beyond the social revolution of the streets. We all know how Prince Albert, who married his cousin Victoria in 1841 and was central to helping her project an image of domestic bliss, 'invented' the Christmas tree in Britain (or at least imported it from Germany). In fact his role in this was merely as a popularizer, rather as was Dickens of Christmas itself, for a nation as mechanically advanced as ours was open to the influence of foreign residents from the dawn of the Industrial Revolution. One result of this was that the families of German merchants were gathering around their Christmas trees in Manchester a couple of decades before the royal family was enjoying them – and since many such traders were Jewish, it is not inconceivable that some of the first Christmas trees in Britain were put up by non-Christians, families influenced more by the custom's links with their old country than by its association with the birth of Christ. Perhaps this is not too incongruous, for so much of the Victorian Christmas was founded on the basis of 'peace on earth and goodwill to all men', a concept that would sit comfortably in any religion or moral code.

The royal family certainly played its part in promoting Christmas, but other factors were crowding in on all sides, seemingly unconnected advances leading to a common end. The post office official Rowland Hill worked long into the night experimenting with glues and pastes, and in 1840 produced the world's first adhesive stamp and the penny pre-paid post. Up until then the recipient paid on delivery, according to how far the letter had travelled, a process which made something of a nonsense of sending a mere message of greeting through the mail. The first Christmas card followed three years later – in 1843, the year of *A Christmas Carol* – designed and sent by the artist H.C. Horsley on the suggestion of his friend Henry Cole. Since Horsley was the brother-in-law of Isambard Kingdom Brunel, we find once again an intriguing link between the glamorization of Christmas and the hard world of commerce – and this trend continued through the century as more advanced printing techniques brought cards within the reach of wider numbers. It was not until the early 1880s, when makers started producing greetings at a few coppers a dozen in the wake of the half-penny postcard post of 1870, that cards began to be exchanged in vast numbers; but it can be said that within fifty years, Horsley's quirky one-off gesture had snowballed into an industry that put severe strain on the national postal service once every twelve months. As for Horsley's brother-in-law, Brunel was just one of the highly influential railway kings who were consigning stagecoaches to history – and at the same time ensuring their immortalization on Christmas cards as sentimental throw-backs to the 'old Christmas'. It was thus that Dickens, too, celebrated this most unsatisfactory form of transport.

As for American writers, several had by this time latched on to the concept of the traditional yuletide. It was certainly from them that the British imported

Santa Claus, the jolly old gentleman who stemmed from the St Nicholas for whom children of Dutch emigrants to New York left out their shoes to be filled with gifts on the eve of his saint's day, 6 December. Washington Irving told of Santa's visit in *Knickerbocker's History of New York* in 1809. In 1821 a periodical published in that city, *The Children's Friend*, carried a story about a visitor arriving in a sleigh drawn by reindeer, and in 1823 a New York State newspaper, the *Troy Sentinel*, set the seal on the rise and rise of Santa by publishing, without the author's permission, the poem 'A

Visit From St Nicholas' (still widely known as 'The Night Before Christmas'). This poem was the work of a New York academic, Clement Clark Moore, and it was written as no more than an entertainment for his children; now it is recited long after his earnest studies into the Hebrew language and Juvenal have been forgotten.

As with the Christmas tree and, indeed, the early cards, the birth of Christ played no part in this slice of seasonal lore. It is interesting to reflect that Horsley's pioneering card of 1843 showed not the Holy family but a typically middle-class gathering sharing drinks, together with vignettes of alms being given to the old, a child and a young woman with a baby. In other words, Horsley had struck upon – or far more likely, simply reflected – the central themes of a Victorian Christmas at a time when he could not possibly have known the contents of Dickens' simultaneously published *A Christmas Carol*. That said, the central character of his card, glass in hand, bears an uncanny resemblance to Phiz's portrayal of Mr Pickwick, who first saw the light of day some half-dozen years earlier, and who so enjoyed Mr Wardle's old-fashioned Christmas hospitality at Dingley Dell.

'Old Christmas' also features strongly in Washington Irving's *Sketch Book* of 1820 in which, writing as the American Geoffrey Crayon abroad in England, he paints a vivid picture of festivities in late Georgian times.

Needless to say, the book was a great success among the reading classes of Britain – although this is a long way from saying that it was anything like universally well known – and it must have been familiar to Dickens long before Mr Pickwick and *A Christmas Carol*. He was also doubtless aware of a short story of 1834 by the then young novelist and political economist Harriet Martineau, in which her heroine told of a country Christmas that 'had always been a season of merriment to her, and to all the household. She always had some cousins to stay with her then . . . and nothing but pleasure was thought of for the whole week.'

The social historians John Golby and William Purdue have carried out fascinating research into the treatment of Christmas in *The Times*. For instance, they quote from a leader article in the newspaper of Christmas 1790 which said: 'within the last half century this annual time of festivity has lost much of its original mirth and hospitality'. Even more revealing, their researches show that in twenty of the years between that date and 1835, *The Times* did not mention Christmas at all; 'for all the remaining years its reports were extremely brief and uninformative'. That was the almost unbelievable background to life before Mr Pickwick burst merrily on to the scene, Washington Irving and Harriet Martineau or not.

No writer loved Christmas more, or exploited it more, than Dickens. As an author and traveller he led a frantically busy life, but from the moment *A Christmas Carol* caught the public's imagination in 1843 a seasonal offering became part of his absurdly heavy annual routine for years to come. At first the emphasis was on full-blown books – *The Chimes* (1844), *The Cricket on the Hearth* (1845), *The Battle of Life* (1846) and *The Haunted Man* (1848). After that he restricted his efforts to Christmas issues of his periodical *Household Words*, where his work was often incorporated into sprawling, multi-faceted stories produced jointly with several other writers. Whatever form his seasonal authorship took, however, most of it was fitted in and around work on the major novels of this, the prime of his writing life, and for this reason it is hardly surprising that the Christmas collection as a group, *A Christmas Carol* apart, does not rank among his most memorable stories.

On the other hand, rarely is Dickens so political, so committed to striking a blow for the toiling masses, as in *The Chimes*. 'All my affections and passions got twined and knotted up in it, and I became as haggard as a murderer long before I wrote The End,' he told one friend. To another he wrote of 'my little Christmas book, in which I have endeavoured to plant an indignant right-hander on the eye of certain wicked Cant that makes my blood boil, which I hope will not only cloud that eye with black and blue, but many a gentle one with crystal of the finest sort'. He was living in Genoa at the time, and to his closest confidant and biographer John Forster he spoke of *The Chimes* making 'my face white in a foreign land. My cheeks, which were beginning to fill out, have sunk again; my eyes have grown immensely large; my hair is very lank; and the head inside the hair is hot and giddy.' Such was the emotion that he put into what is now dismissed by many as one of the least notable of his works.

In contrast, *A Christmas Carol* was seen from the start as a masterpiece. 'You have done more good by this little publication, fostered more kindly feelings and prompted more kindly acts of beneficence than can be traced to all the pulpits and confessionals in Christendom since Christmas 1842,' he was told by Francis, Lord Jeffrey. And in *Fraser's Magazine* in July 1844, the normally astringent critic Thackeray wrote:

Who can listen to objections regarding such a book as this? It seems to me a national benefit, and to every man or woman who reads it a personal kindness. The last two people I heard speak of it were women; neither knew the other, or the author, and both said, by way of criticism, 'God bless him'. As for Tiny Tim, there is a passage in the book regarding that young gentleman about which a man should hardly venture to speak in print or in public, any more than he would any other affections of his private heart. There is not a reader in England but that little creature will be a bond of union between the author and him; and he will say of Charles Dickens, as the women just now, 'God bless him'. A Scotch philosopher, who nationally does not keep Christmas Day, on reading the

book sent out for a turkey, and asked two friends to dinner . . . What a feeling is this for a writer to be able to inspire, and what a reward to reap!

Ah yes, rewards. Almost as many people who know that *A Christmas Carol* was a sensation from day one are equally well aware of the disappointment its first royalties caused the author. Chapman & Hall's initial print run of 6,000 was priced at five shillings – no great sum, in those days before mass production, to pay for a handsome volume of 166 pages that included four coloured illustrations and four woodcuts by John Leech. The result was a profit alarmingly lower than Dickens had expected. 'Such a night as I have passed!' he wrote to Forster in the following February. 'I really believed I should never get up again, until I had passed through all the horrors of a fever. I found the *Carol* accounts awaiting me, and they were the cause of it. The first six thousand copies show a profit of £230. And the last four [thousand] will yield as much more. I had set my heart and soul upon a Thousand clear.'

Such was Charles Dickens' first commercial experience of the greatest of all his Christmas books. They were works produced against a personal background that did not necessarily allow for Christmases of domestic bliss, for as his children increased and his affection switched increasingly from his wife to another woman, his life was scarcely recognizable as a model of upright Victorian rectitude. But though money and material success were important to him – they had to be in the light of the complicated and expensive life he led – he knew that there was more to his specifically seasonal writings than pot-boiling alone. *A Christmas Carol* apart, they do not rank among his major works. But he was always true to himself in them, always meant what he wrote, and the life force and commitment that informed them then still blaze forth today.

Oh the Grocers'!

Charles Dickens

Dickens loved describing the bustle of the festive season. Unashamed commercialism was very much a part of his Christmas. Here the Ghost of Christmas Present shows the reality of life beyond his gloomy lodgings – and gives Dickens the opportunity to indulge in one of his favourite pursuits, describing shops bulging with produce.

The poulterers' shops were still half open, and the fruiterers' were radiant in their glory. There were great, round, pot-bellied baskets of chestnuts, shaped like the waistcoats of jolly old gentlemen, lolling at the doors, and tumbling out into the street in their apoplectic opulence. There were ruddy, brown-faced broad-girthed Spanish Onions, shining in the fatness of their growth like Spanish Friars; and winking from their shelves in wanton slyness at the girls as they went by, and glancing demurely at the hung-up mistletoe. There were pears and apples, clustered high in blooming pyramids; there were bunches of grapes, made, in the shopkeepers' benevolence, to dangle from conspicuous hooks, that people's mouths might water gratis as they passed; there were piles of filberts, mossy and brown, recalling, in their fragrance, ancient walks among the woods, and pleasant shufflings ankle deep through withered leaves; there were Norfolk Biffins, squab, and swarthy, setting off the yellow of the oranges and lemons, and, in the great compactness of their juicy persons, urgently entreating and beseeching to be carried home in paper bags and eaten after dinner. The very gold and silver fish, set forth among these choice fruits in a bowl, though members of a dull and stagnant-blooded race, appeared to know that there was something going on; and, to a fish, went gasping round and round their little world in slow and passionless excitement.

The Grocers'! Oh the Grocers'! Nearly closed, with perhaps two shutters down, or one; but through those gaps such glimpses! It was not alone that the scales descending on the counter made a merry sound, or that the twine and roller parted company so briskly, or that the canisters were rattled up and down like juggling tricks, or even that the blended scents of tea and coffee were so grateful to the nose, or even that the raisins were so plentiful and rare, the almonds so extremely white, the sticks of cinnamon so long and straight, the other spices so delicious, the candied fruits so caked and spotted with molten sugar as to make the coldest lookers-on feel faint and subsequently bilious. Nor was it that the figs were moist and pulpy, or that the French plums blushed in modest tartness from their highly-decorated boxes, or that everything was good to eat and in its Christmas dress: but the customers were all so hurried and so eager in the hopeful promise of the day, that they tumbled up against each other at the door, clashing their wicker baskets wildly, and left their purchases upon the counter, and came running back to fetch them, and committed hundreds of the like mistakes in the best humour possible; while the Grocer and his people were so frank and fresh that the polished hearts with which they fastened their aprons behind might have been their own, worn outside for general inspection, and for Christmas daws to peck at if they chose.

Bracebridge Hall

Washington Irving

Writing as Geoffrey Crayon, the American Washington Irving produced two books, The Sketch Book *in 1820 and the collection of essays* Bracebridge Hall *in 1822, that must have influenced Dickens' perception of Christmas; interesting to reflect that a man from the New World did so much to revive interest in the old English country Christmas.*

The world has become more worldly. There is more of dissipation, and less of enjoyment. Pleasure has expanded into a broader but shallower stream and has forsaken many of those deep and quiet channels where it flowed sweetly through the calm bosom of domestic life. Society has acquired a more enlightened and elegant tone, but it has lost many of its peculiarities, its home-bred feelings, its honest fireside delights. The traditional customs of golden hearted antiquity. Its feudal hospitalities and lordly wassailings have passed away with the baronial castles and the stately manor-houses in which they were celebrated. They comported with the shadowy hall, the great oaken gallery and the tapestried parlour, but are unfitted in the light showy saloons and gay drawing rooms of the modern villa.

Shorn, however, as it is, of its ancient and festive honours, Christmas is still a period of delightful excitement in England. It is gratifying to see that home feeling completely aroused which holds so powerful a place in every English bosom. The preparations making on every side for the social board that is again to unite friends and kindred; the presents of good cheer passing and repassing, those tokens of regard, and quickeners of kind feelings; the evergreens distributed about houses and churches, emblems of peace and gladness: all these have the most pleasing effect in producing fond associations, and kindling benevolent sympathies. Even the sound of the Waits, rude as may be their minstrelsy, breaks up the midwatch of a winter's night with the effect of perfect harmony. As I have been awakened by them in that still and solemn hour, 'when deep sleep falleth upon man', I have listened with a hushed delight, and connecting them with the sacred and joyous occasion, have almost fancied them into another celestial choir, announcing peace and goodwill to mankind.

* * *

In the course of a December tour in Yorkshire, I rode for a long distance in one of the public coaches, on the day preceding Christmas. The coach was crowded, both inside and out, with passengers who, by their talk, seemed principally bound to the mansions of relations or friends, to eat Christmas dinner. It was loaded also with hampers of game, and baskets and boxes of delicacies; and hares hung dangling their long ears about the coachman's box, presents from distant friends for the impending feast.

I had three rosy-cheeked boys for my fellow passengers inside, full of the buxom health which I have observed in the children of this country. They were returning home for the holidays in high glee, and promising themselves a world of enjoyment. It was delightful to hear the gigantic plans of the little rogues . . .

They were under the particular guardianship of the coachman, to whom, whenever an opportunity presented itself, they addressed a host of questions, and pronounced him one of the best fellows in the world. Indeed I could not but notice the more than ordinary air of bustle and importance of the coachman, who wore his hat on one side, and had a large bunch of Christmas greens stuck in the buttonhole of his coat. He is always a personage full of mighty care and business, but he is particularly so this season having so many commissions to execute in consequence of the great interchange of presents. And here, perhaps, it may not be unacceptable to my untravelled readers to have a sketch that may serve as a general representation of this very numerous and important class of functionaries, who have a dress, a manner, a language, and air peculiar to themselves and prevalent throughout the fraternity, so that wherever an English stage coachman may be seen he cannot be mistaken for one of any other craft or mystery.

He has commonly, a broad, full face, curiously mottled with red, as if the blood has been forced by hard feeding into every vessel of the skin; he is swelled into jolly dimensions by frequent potations of malt liquors, and his bulk is still further increased by a multiplicity of coats in which he is buried like a cauliflower . . . He wears a broad brimmed low crowned hat, a huge roll of coloured handkerchief around his neck . . . His waistcoat is commonly of some bright colour, and his small clothes extend far below the knees to meet with a pair of jocky boots . . .

A stagecoach carries animation along with it . . . The horn, sounded at the entrance to a village, produces a general bustle. Some hasten forth to meet friends, some with bundles and bandboxes to secure places, and in the hurry of the moment can hardly take leave of the group that accompanies them. In the meantime the coachman has a world of small commissions to exercise . . .

Perhaps the impending holiday might have given a more than usual animation to the country . . . Game, poultry, and other luxuries for the table, were in brisk circulation in the villages; the grocers', butchers' and fruiterers' shops were thronged with customers. The housewives were stirring briskly about putting their dwellings in order; and the glossy branches of holly, with their bright red berries, began to appear at the windows . . .

In the evening we reached a village where I was determined to pass the night. As we drove into the great gateway of the Inn, I saw on one side the light of a rousing kitchen fire beaming through a window. I entered, and admired for the hundredth time, that picture of convenience, neatness, and broad honest enjoyment, the kitchen of an English Inn. It was of spacious dimensions, hung round with copper and tin vessels highly polished, and decorated here and there with a Christmas green. Hams, tongues and flitches of bacon were suspended from the ceiling; a smoke jack made its ceaseless clanking beside the fireplace, and a clock ticked in one corner. A well-scoured deal table extended along one side of the kitchen, with a cold round of beef and other viands upon it, over which two foaming tankards of ale seemed mounting guard. Travellers of inferior order were preparing to attack this stout repast, while others sat smoking and gossiping over their ale on two high back oaken settles beside the fire . . .

I had not been long at the inn when a post-chaise drove up to the door. A young gentleman stepped out. It was Frank Bracebridge, a sprightly, good humoured fellow with whom I had once travelled on the Continent. He insisted that I should give him a day or two at his father's country seat. 'It is better than eating a solitary Christmas dinner at an inn,' said he, 'and I can assure you of a hearty welcome in something of the old fashioned style.' I closed therefore at once, with his invitation; the chaise drove to the door, and in a few moments I was on my way to the family mansion of the Bracebridges . . .

* * *

It was a brilliant moonlight night, but extremely cold; the chaise whirled rapidly over the frozen ground . . . As we approached the house, we heard the sound of music, and now and then a burst of laughter, from one end of the building. This, Bracebridge said, must proceed from the servants' hall, where a great deal of revelry was permitted, and even encouraged by the squire, throughout the twelve days of Christmas, provided everything was done conformably to ancient usage. Here were kept up the old games of Hoodman Blind, shoe the wild mare, hot cockles, steal the white loaf, bob apple, and snap dragon; the Yule log and Christmas candle were regularly burnt, and the mistletoe with its white berries, hung up, to the imminent peril of all the pretty housemaids . . .

Supper was announced shortly after our arrival. It was served up in a spacious oaken chamber, the panels of which shone with wax and around which were several family portraits decorated with Holly and Ivy. Besides

The artist Caldecott's impression of the great Christmas feast at Bracebridge Hall.

the accustomed lights, two great wax tapers, called Christmas candles, wreathed with greens, were placed on a high polished buffet among the family plate. The table was abundantly spread with substantial fare; but the squire made his supper of frumenty, a dish made of wheat cakes boiled in milk, with rich spices . . .

I was happy to find my old friend Minc'd Pie in the retinue of the feast; and finding him to be perfectly orthodox, and that I need not be ashamed of my predilection, I greeted him with all the warmth wherewith we usually greet an old and very genteel acquaintance . . .

Medieval revels, Victorian style, add to the gaiety at Bracebridge Hall.

The supper had disposed everyone to gaiety, and an old harper was summoned from the servants' hall . . . The dance, like most dances after supper, was a merry one; some of the older folk joined in it, and the squire himself figured down several couple with a partner, with whom he affirmed he had danced every Christmas for nearly half a century. Master Simon, who seemed to be a connecting link between the old times and the new, and to be withal a little antiquated with the tastes of his accomplishments, evidently piqued himself on his dancing and was attempting to gain credit by the heel toe rigadoon, and other graces of the ancient school; but he had unluckily assorted himself with a little romping girl from boarding school, who, by her wild vivacity, kept him continually on the stretch and defeated all his sober attempts at elegance . . .

The young Oxonian, on the contrary, had led out one of his maiden aunts, on whom the rogue played a thousand little knaveries with impunity: he was full of practical jokes and his delight was to tease his aunts and cousins. The most interesting couple in the dance was the young officer and a ward of the squire's, a beautiful, blushing girl of seventeen. From several shy glances which I had noticed in the course of the evening, I suspected there was a little kindness growing up between them; and indeed, the young soldier was just the hero to captivate a romantic girl. He was tall, slender and handsome, and, like most of the young British officers of late years, had picked up various small accomplishments on the Continent: he could talk French and Italian, draw landscapes, sing very tolerably, dance divinely; but above all, he had been wounded at Waterloo: what girl of seventeen well read in poetry and romance, could resist such a mirror of chivalry and perfection . . .

The party now broke up for the night with the kindhearted old custom of shaking hands. As I passed through the hall on the way to my chamber, the dying embers of the Yule log still sent forth a dusky glow, and had it not been 'the season when no spirit dares stir abroad', I should have been half tempted to steal from my room at midnight, and peep whether the fairies might not be at their revels about the hearth . . .

I had scarcely got into bed when a strain of music seemed to break forth in the air just below the window. I listened, and found it proceeded from a band, which I concluded to be the Waits from some neighbouring village. They went round the house playing under the windows. I drew aside the curtains to hear them more distinctly. The sounds as they receded, became more soft and aerial, and seemed to accord with the quiet and the moonlight. I listened and listened; they became more and more tender and remote, and, as they gradually died away, my head sunk upon the pillow, and I fell asleep.

* * *

When I awoke the next morning, it seemed as if all the events of the preceding evening had been a dream, and nothing but the identity of the ancient chamber in which I lay convinced me of their reality . . . While I lay musing on my pillows I heard the sound of little feet pattering outside of the door, and a whispering consultation. Presently a choir of small voices chanted forth an old Christmas carol, the burden of which was,

> Rejoice our Saviour he was born
> On Christmas day in the morning.

I rose softly, slipped on my clothes, opened the door suddenly, and beheld one of the most beautiful little fairy groups that a painter could imagine. It consisted of a boy and two girls, the eldest not more than six, and lovely as seraphs. They were going the rounds of the house, and singing at every chamber door; but my sudden appearance frightened them into mute bashfulness. They remained for a moment playing on their lips with their fingers, and now and then stealing a shy glance from under their eyebrows, until, as if by one impulse, they scampered away, and as they turned on the angle of the gallery, I heard them laughing in triumph at their escape.

* * *

A few years before he had kept open house during the holidays in the old style. The country people, however, did not understand how to play their parts in the scene of hospitality; many uncouth circumstances occurred; the manor was overrun by all the vagrants of the country, and more beggars drawn into the neighbourhood in one week than the parish officers could get rid of in a year. Since then, he had contented himself with inviting the decent part of the neighbouring peasantry to call at the hall on Christmas day, and with distributing beef, and bread, and ale, among the poor, that they might make merry in their own dwellings.

We had not been long home when the sound of music was heard from a distance. A band of country lads, without coats, their shirt sleeves fancifully tied with ribbons, their hats decorated with greens, and clubs in their hands, were seen advancing up the avenue, followed by a large number of villagers and peasantry. They stopped before the hall door, where the music struck up a peculiar air, and the lads performed a curious and intricate dance, advancing, retreating and striking their clubs together, keeping exact time to the music; while one, whimsically crowned with a fox's skin, the tail of which flaunted down his back, kept capering round the skirts of the dance, and rattling a Christmas box with many antic gesticulations.

Kissed by Every One

Charles Dickens

Nowhere is the old-fashioned Christmas of Dickens' childhood – or more precisely, from folk memories handed down to him by his elders – more happily encapsulated than in the festivities at Dingley Dell in his first novel The Pickwick Papers. *Dickens, born in 1812, completed the book between 1836 and '37.*

From the centre of the ceiling of this kitchen, old Wardle had just suspended, with his own hands, a huge branch of mistletoe, and this same branch of mistletoe instantaneously gave rise to a scene of general and most delightful struggling and confusion; in the midst of which, Mr Pickwick, with a gallantry that would have done honour to a descendant of Lady Tollimglower herself, took the old lady by the hand, led her beneath the mystic branch, and saluted her in all courtesy and decorum. The old lady submitted to this piece of practical politeness with all the dignity which befitted so important and serious a solemnity, but the younger ladies, not being so thoroughly imbued with a superstitious veneration for the custom, or imagining that the value of a salute is very much enhanced if it cost a little trouble to obtain it, screamed and struggled, and ran into corners, and threatened and remonstrated, and did everything but leave the room, until some of the less adventurous gentlemen were on the point of desisting, when they all at once found it useless to resist any longer, and submitted to be kissed with a good grace.

Mr Winkle kissed the young lady with the black eyes, and Mr Snodgrass kissed Emily, and Mr Weller, not being particular about the form of being under the mistletoe, kissed Emma and the other female servants, just as he caught them. As to the poor relations, they kissed everybody, not even excepting the plainer portion of the young-lady visitors, who, in their excessive confusion, ran right under the mistletoe as soon as it was hung up, without knowing it! Wardle stood with his back to the fire, surveying the whole scene with the utmost satisfaction; and the fat boy took the opportunity of appropriating to his own use, and summarily devouring, a particularly fine mince-pie, that had been carefully put by for somebody else.

Now, the screaming had subsided, and faces were in a glow, and curls in a tangle, and Mr Pickwick, after kissing the old lady, as before mentioned, was standing under the mistletoe, looking with a very pleased countenance on all that was passing around him, when the young lady with the black eyes, after a little whispering with the other young ladies, made a sudden dart forward, and putting her arm round Mr Pickwick's neck, saluted him affectionately on the left cheek; and before Mr Pickwick distinctly knew what was the matter, he was surrounded by the whole body, and kissed by every one of them.

It was a pleasant thing to see Mr Pickwick in the centre of the group, now pulled this way, and then that, and first kissed on the chin, and then on the nose, and then on the spectacles: and to hear the peals of laughter which were raised on every side; but it was a still more pleasant thing to see Mr Pickwick, blinded shortly afterwards with a silk handkerchief, falling up

'Before Mr Pickwick distinctly knew what was the matter, he was surrounded by the whole body, and kissed by every one of them.'

against the wall, and scrambling into corners, and going through all the mysteries of blind-man's buff, with the utmost relish for the game, until at last he caught one of the poor relations, and then had to evade the blind-man himself, which he did with a nimbleness and agility that elicited the admiration and applause of all beholders. The poor relations caught the people who they thought would like it; and when the game flagged, got caught themselves. When they were all tired of blind-man's buff, there was a great game at snap-dragon, and when fingers enough were burned with that, and all the raisins were gone, they sat down, by the huge fire of blazing logs, to a substantial supper, and a mighty bowl of wassail, something smaller than an ordinary wash-house copper, in which the hot apples were hissing and bubbling with a rich look, and a jolly sound, that were perfectly irresistible.

'This,' said Mr Pickwick, looking round him, 'this is, indeed, comfort.'

'Our invariable custom,' replied Mr Wardle. 'Everybody sits down with us on Christmas-eve, as you see them now – servants and all; and here we wait, until the clock strikes twelve, to usher Christmas in, and beguile the time with forfeits and old stories. Trundle, my boy, rake up the fire.'

Up flew the bright sparks in myriads as the logs were stirred. The deep red blaze sent forth a rich glow, that penetrated into the furthest corner of the room, and cast its cheerful tint on every face.

'Come,' said Wardle, 'a song – a Christmas song! I'll give you one, in default of a better.'

'Bravo!' said Mr Pickwick.

'Fill up,' cried Wardle. 'It will be two hours, good, before you see the bottom of the bowl through the deep rich colour of the wassail; fill up, all round, and now for the song.'

Thus saying, the merry old gentleman, in a good, round, sturdy voice, commenced without more ado:

> I care not for Spring; on his fickle wing
> Let the blossoms and buds be borne:
> He woos them amain with his treacherous rain,
> And he scatters them ere the morn.
> An inconstant elf, he knows not himself,
> Nor his own changing mind an hour,
> He'll smile in your face, and with wry grimace,
> He'll wither your youngest flower.

Let the Summer sun to his bright home run,
He shall never be sought by me;
When he's dimmed by a cloud I can laugh aloud,
And care not how sulky he be!
For his darling child is the madness wild
That sports in fierce fever's train;
And when love is too strong, it don't last long,
As many have found to their pain.

A mild harvest night, by the tranquil light
Of the modest and gentle moon,
Has a far sweeter sheen, for me, I ween,
Than the broad and unblushing noon.
But every leaf awakens my grief,
As it lieth beneath the tree;
So let Autumn air be never so fair,
It by no means agrees with me.

But my song I troll out, for CHRISTMAS stout,
The hearty, the true, and the bold;
A bumper I drain, and with might and main
Give three cheers for this Christmas old!
We'll usher him in with a merry din
That shall gladden his joyous heart,
And we'll keep him up, while there's bite or sup,
And in fellowship good, we'll part.

In his fine honest pride, he scorns to hide
One jot of his hard-weather scars;
They're no disgrace, for there's much the same trace
On the cheeks of our bravest tars.
Then again I sing till the roof doth ring,
And it echoes from wall to wall –
To the stout old wight, fair welcome to-night,
As the King of the Seasons all!

This song was tumultuously applauded – for friends and dependants make a
capital audience – and the poor relations, especially, were in perfect ecstasies
of rapture. Again was the fire replenished, and again went the wassail round.

Notes for Kind Hosts

Phillis Browne

Rough boys at one end of the room, shy girls at the other . . . many of us who grew up in the post-war years will remember children's parties that started like that. These tips, from an article titled 'How to Give a Children's Party', come from a Christmas issue of Cassell's Family Magazine *of Victorian times.*

It is of no use to expect that when the children have arrived they will amuse themselves. They will not. If left to do so, the boys will gradually collect in one part of the room, and, I am afraid, will sometimes conduct themselves rather roughly; and the girls will sit modestly and silently in another part, scarcely speaking a word. It needs a grown-up person possessed of both energy and kindliness, and who has made up his or her mind that hard work will be required both to begin the enjoyment and to keep it up. It is the best thing to draw up a programme beforehand, and to have all the details arranged; and it requires forethought and care to see that there is no hitch in them. Of course the most delightful plan is to have a special entertainment provided for the children – a conjurer to puzzle them, or a show of some kind for them to watch. It is not every one, however, who can afford to pay a professional person to undertake the management of it; and it must be properly carried out, or it is worse than nothing.

What can be more wearisome than to sit in a darkened room watching an inexperienced amateur try to exhibit a magic lantern? An oily smell, suggestive of headache, fills the apartment; the spectators are anxiously waiting for the sight, when a black figure is seen to rush through the darkness, to seek somewhere for something which has been forgotten, and which is not found, and for want of which the pictures look like nothing but an illuminated haze, indistinct and unsatisfactory. The politer members of the company do their best to admire, but at the same time feel immensely relieved when the impracticable machine is removed, and an ordinary round game is called for.

Of late years Christmas-trees have become very popular at children's parties. They are exceedingly pretty, and when tastefully trimmed with glittering ornaments, and lighted up with small lamps or candles, have a very charming appearance. When more than this is attempted, however, I think they are a mistake. Ticketed presents for the children are often hung upon the tree, and corresponding tickets drawn for. I have scarcely ever known this plan successful. In nine cases out of ten the boys get the dolls, and the girls the cricket-balls; and one difference between children and grown-up people is that the former find more difficulty in hiding their feelings than the latter. The kind host and hostess give themselves a great deal of trouble, and put themselves to expense, and after all only succeed in making their guests discontented and dissatisfied.

If it is wished to make presents to the children, why not have a bran-pie?

That is, a large box filled with bran, in which is hidden a present specially designed for each child, and marked with his name, and which is sought for by the youngest guest present. Or let one of the grown-up people dress like an old man, and come in laden with the treasures. All sorts of similar plans might be adopted, but it is not well to leave the distribution of the presents to chance.

One of the most successful parties that my children ever attended was given by a clever and rather eccentric friend of mine. In issuing her invitations, she requested that the children might arrive not later than three, and be sent for not later than eight o'clock. When they arrived, they were shown into a large, comfortable room, and the hostess and a lady friend joined with them in playing at old-fashioned round games, which were continued after tea. About half-past seven the children were taken into another room, and invited to seat themselves round a large table. In the middle of this was a Christmas-tree, prettily lighted and tastefully decorated. A place was set for each child upon which was an orange, a piece of cake, and a few raisins, and by the side of the plate a small parcel containing a present. Upon the parcel was placed a doll's candlestick holding a small wax taper, lighted. The children examined their presents and partook of their refreshment by the light only of the candles and the Christmas-tree, and their delight was unbounded.

There is one word that must be said to parents in speaking of children's parties. When children receive an invitation to a party, the object of those who give it can only be either to give pleasure to the children, or to compliment the parents. In return for this they have a right to expect that they shall be treated fairly. This cannot be said to be the case if the children when they leave home are not perfectly well. So many of the complaints peculiar to children are spread by carelessness of this kind; and what can be more annoying to a host and hostess than to find that their house has been the centre from which illness has spread to their friends?

Bah! Humbug!

Charles Dickens

*Bogart and Bergman never said 'Play it again, Sam'. Cagney never said
'You dirty rat'. Yet this extract from* A Christmas Carol *gives us proof
positive that Scrooge really did say 'Bah! Humbug!' when confronted by
his determinedly cheery nephew in his counting house.*

Once upon a time – of all the good days in the year, on Christmas Eve –
old Scrooge sat busy in his counting-house. It was cold, bleak, biting
weather: foggy withal: and he could hear the people in the court outside go
wheezing up and down, beating their hands upon their breasts, and stamping
their feet upon the pavement-stones to warm them. The City clocks had only
just gone three, but it was quite dark already: it had not been light all day;
and candles were flaring in the windows of the neighbouring offices, like
ruddy smears upon the palpable brown air. The fog came pouring in at every
chink and keyhole, and was so dense without, that although the court was of
the narrowest, the houses opposite were mere phantoms. To see the dingy
cloud come drooping down, obscuring everything, one might have thought
that Nature lived hard by, and was brewing on a large scale.

The door of Scrooge's counting-house was open that he might keep his
eye upon his clerk, who in a dismal little cell beyond, a sort of tank, was
copying letters. Scrooge had a very small fire, but the clerk's fire was so very
much smaller that it looked like one coal. But he couldn't replenish it, for
Scrooge kept the coal-box in his own room; and so surely as the clerk came
in with the shovel, the master predicted that it would be necessary for them
to part. Wherefore the clerk put on his white comforter, and tried to warm
himself at the candle; in which effort, not being a man of a strong
imagination, he failed.

'A merry Christmas, uncle! God save you!' cried a cheerful voice. It was
the voice of Scrooge's nephew, who came upon him so quickly that this was
the first intimation he had of his approach.

'Bah!' said Scrooge, 'Humbug!'

He had so heated himself with rapid walking in the fog and frost, this nephew of Scrooge's, that he was all in a glow; his face was ruddy and handsome; his eyes sparkled, and his breath smoked again.

'Christmas a humbug, uncle!' said Scrooge's nephew. 'You don't mean that, I am sure.'

'I do,' said Scrooge. 'Merry Christmas! What right have you to be merry? What reason have you to be merry? You're poor enough.'

'Come, then,' returned the nephew gaily. 'What right have you to be dismal? What reason have you to be morose? You're rich enough.'

Scrooge having no better answer ready on the spur of the moment, said, 'Bah!' again; and followed it up with 'Humbug.'

'Don't be cross, uncle,' said the nephew.

'What else can I be,' returned the uncle, 'when I live in such a world of fools as this? Merry Christmas! Out upon merry Christmas! What's Christmas time to you but a time for paying bills without money; a time for finding yourself a year older, but not an hour richer; a time for balancing your books and having every item in 'em through a round dozen of months presented dead against you? If I could work my will,' said Scrooge, indignantly, 'every idiot who goes about with "Merry Christmas" on his lips, should be boiled with his own pudding, and buried with a stake of holly through his heart. He should!'

'Uncle!' pleaded the nephew.

'Nephew!' returned the uncle, sternly, 'keep Christmas in your own way, and let me keep it in mine.'

'Keep it!' repeated Scrooge's nephew. 'But you don't keep it.'

'Let me leave it alone, then,' said Scrooge. 'Much good may it do you! Much good it has ever done you!'

'There are many things from which I might have derived good, by which I have not profited, I dare say,' returned the nephew: 'Christmas among the rest. But I am sure I have always thought of Christmas time, when it has come round – apart from the veneration due to its sacred name and origin, if anything belonging to it can be apart from that – as a good time: a kind, forgiving, charitable, pleasant time: the only time I know of, in the long calendar of the year, when men and women seem by one consent to open their shut-up hearts freely, and to think of people below them as if they really were fellow-passengers to the grave, and not another race of creatures bound on other journeys. And therefore, uncle, though it has never put a scrap of gold or silver in my pocket, I believe that it has done me good, and will do me good; and I say, God bless it!'

Christmas and New Year Presents

From Little Folks *magazine, these hints on making presents for loved ones tell us much about the Victorians' expectations of patience and skill in their children.*

As I sit down to write this little paper on some easily-made presents, Christmas and the New Year are fast approaching.

There are few homes where they are not looked forward to as times of present giving and receiving by old and young alike; for the old folks love to make the time a season of happiness to those around, that the young may some day look back on it as a bright memory never to be forgotten.

There are several merry ways and means of giving presents, and a few need but be mentioned to help many a bright-faced circle at once to set to work for the happy time. Christmas-trees we are all almost tired of, though they still delight very little folk. As everyone knows how to decorate them, only three suggestions on that subject are necessary. Firstly, the trees look much more wintry and Christmas-like if new cotton wool is laid along the tops of their branches (always a difficult place to dress), to imitate snow; secondly, a snake cut out of a round piece of cardboard, and gilded, when carefully balanced on a large pin stuck into the very top of the tree, where the heat of the candles will make it revolve all the time, looks very well; thirdly, numbers of very small penny dolls (about two inches long), dressed in some very sparkling material, with shiny gauze wings, and hung about the dark parts of the tree, add wonderfully to its attractiveness.

A Christmas post-office is a merry-making idea in which all can join, from the oldest to the youngest, for even grandpapa and grandmamma like to get a Christmas letter. To do this, you must rail off with screens one large corner of the room where you intend to have it; these you can adorn with holly and other evergreens, one small opening being left, across which you put a little table. Hang up a cloth or shawl over the upper part, letting it come down just low enough to make a small square aperture, about the size of a railway ticket-office window. Behind this sits the post-mistress, and whoever goes to inquire for a letter is sure to get one addressed to them. In it they find a number, which, on showing at another large window (that should be made at the side of the office), is exchanged for a parcel bearing the same figure. Some people's correspondence is very large, and as many as thirteen or fourteen letters fall to the share of one person.

The amusement that is the prettiest way of giving presents is that of the period when Christmas was called 'Yule-tide', and people burnt enormous Yule-logs, at which they roasted oxen and sheep whole; those may have been to a certain degree 'the good old times', but they were undoubtedly very rough and uncomfortable when compared with our modern days. 'Yule-traps' is, however, a part of the old customs that we may still keep up, as it gives great amusement. It consists in hiding one present in another, disguising it in such a manner as to test the cleverness of the receiver not a little in finding it out.

For example, a soft pair of kid gloves can be rolled up, and secured in a large Spanish walnut-shell previously emptied, and the two halves gummed together; a case of knitting-needles will be hidden in what appears to be nothing but a flat block of wood, which, by a little knowledge of simple carpentering can be made to slide into two pieces so as to discover it. A little pot of damson cheese has been found to have the preserve dexterously cut away underneath, sufficiently to give room for the pot to contain also a delicate gold chain or ornament. A large pair of swede turnips has been made the holder of a present of game – and so on; any one with a little ingenuity can invent traps by the dozen, and the more peculiar they are, the greater the fun. The amusement may be still further increased by hiding the traps or presents all about the sitting-rooms of the house.

Now as to the presents themselves. It is always pleasant to be able to buy any we like, but nearly every one values more a gift that has been specially made for them than the smartest bought thing. So, little folk, let us set to work to think what we can make, how it is to be done, and for whom.

We ought to begin with grandpapa, who must have a warm pair of slippers of either knitted or wool work, and to show these off well he should be able to put his feet on a pretty round footstool, embroidered or braided for his use. One of the boys might carve him a paper-knife out of a piece of sandal-wood, with a fretwork handle; and a grand-daughter could net or crochet him a long purse.

Grandmamma loves a warm quilted cape of some dark silk edged with fur, which one of the elder girls might make for her, whilst the little folk, with card tastefully painted, and bound with ribbon, can make a case for her spectacles or ball of wool when knitting; or a large pincushion for her dressing-table, trimmed with lace, and with ribbons curled in bunches at the corners.

Papa likes a fretwork writing-case for his table, which the boys can make, mounting it neatly on leather, and putting in blotting-paper afterwards; or a pair of warm knitted glove-mittens, manufactured by one of his little daughters.

For mamma there are many pretty things. The boys can give her ornamental brackets for her room, or frames for their own and sisters' photographs; the elder sister should make her a lovely white satin sachet for her pocket-handkerchiefs, whilst the younger ones might accomplish a glove-box of painted card, wadded, and bound with ribbon.

Amongst the presents which deft-fingered older little folk can invent for each other are some of the following: glove or handkerchief boxes (made of tinted or white card), paper and music cases, or work-baskets and spill-jars, all of which should be adorned by painting outside, and bound with bright-coloured ribbon. Spill-jars can be made by taking a piece of card about seven inches long by five and a half wide, and joining it very exactly, gumming one side a little bit over the other, so as to form a cylinder, and when dry, binding it neatly top and bottom with narrow ribbon. Cut out a perfectly round piece of card the size of the cylinder, and having bound that also, sew its edges with tiny stitches to the edges of the bottom of the jar, and it will be finished. You can make very pretty ones by painting them black, and putting sprays of dried leaves on them.

Nice writing-cases can be made of American cloth, stiffened with card, and lined with brown holland or silk, bound at the edges with strong ribbon; the whole thing to be folded up, and secured with an elastic band. Pocket work-cases, for holding cotton, needles, thimble, and scissors, may be also made of American cloth, lined with silk.

Ornamental boxes filled with paper and envelopes, on which initial letters, monograms, or flowers have been painted, are always useful.

Boys often like to make a collection of stamps or monograms, and a book begun with some finished and half-finished designs for arranging them in is very acceptable, as is also a book made of flannel for keeping fishing-flies.

Again, a little cabinet with drawers, nicely marked out in divisions, containing the beginning of a collection of coins, minerals, sea-shells, or any other curiosities, gives much pleasure, and often leads a lad to take interest in the fairy realms of nature. Some little girls are fond of copying and keeping favourite pieces of poetry, therefore a book commenced with carefully drawn and painted borders of flowers, arabesques, or illuminations is a very welcome gift. Small botanical collections of sea-weed, flowers, ferns, or those most beautiful but little-thought-of plants, mosses, are a continual source of amusement.

Little girls who are clever with their needles may quickly make an exceedingly pretty apron thus: On a nice piece of black or dark silk or satin, lay across the lower half a variety of narrow coloured ribbons, some having a pattern on them. Work down their edges with silk braids, or feather-stitch in different and contrasting-coloured silks, also work in the middle of them fancy stitches, like stars, rounds, or crosses. When made up the effect is very bright and pretty. If there are pockets they should be trimmed in the same way.

Wicker-work baskets, when of a graceful shape, can be beautified by laying on a little way from the edge a two-inch crimped silk fringe in two colours, say pink or blue laid over white. The inside lining of blue or pink silk or satin must be either drawn up in a bag shape, or made into dainty pockets, with little ribbon bows on each. The handle must be decorated with the same fringes, which give the whole basket a soft, fluffy appearance.

Those who can make dolls' clothes have many chances of giving acceptable presents, for a dollie with a complete wardrobe is most fascinating to any little girl, and a pleasant variety is made by dressing dolls in historical or foreign costumes.

Brush and shoe bags made in common crash, and embroidered in crewels with flowers or initials, are useful to every one, and even boys might manufacture them. As they all ought certainly to know how to net, and make artificial flies, they can always give a landing-net or book of flies to their young fishermen friends, who highly prize such treasures.

Pincushions, mats, pen-wipers, and needle-books have not been mentioned, for they are generally almost troublesome by their numbers. It is, indeed, hardly necessary to enumerate more presents, for once ingenuity and invention are set working ideas come so fast that the Christmas cupboard or drawer is rapidly filled.

A Market for Christmas

In 1985 Raymond Hargreaves published Victorian Years, Bolton 1850–60 *(Ross Anderson Publications), an engrossing portrait of a decade in the life of a Lancashire town at the heart of the Industrial Revolution. His narrative was built up by quoting verbatim the* Bolton Chronicle *newspaper, and this report takes us back to 22 December 1855, the year after Dickens had published* Hard Times, *which he set in that part of England. So many Dickensian themes emerge in this straightforward newspaper account: the workers allowed to glimpse the splendour of the occasion of the opening of the market hall, the ball for the elite, the merry souls rolling up in the hope of dancing, but finding the hall too crowded; even the pickpockets. By coincidence, Bolton figured dolefully in Dickens' life in 1869, the year before his death, when he felt dizzy during a public reading there and was forced to abandon his last tour of the North; life was never the same for him after that – but on a happier note, it is pleasant to reflect that, like* Hard Times, *the hall is a product of the 1850s that has survived to this day. Painstakingly refurbished, it stands at the heart of a new shopping complex.*

Bolton, within the last few years, has risen greatly in population, wealth and importance, and so rapidly have its material improvements succeeded each other that a stranger who knew the town 20 years ago would scarcely be able to recognise it. New churches, new institutions, public offices and a new bank rival each other in taste and architectural display, and the new and splendid Market Hall, whose public opening we record below, crowns the whole with classic purity and magnificence. In point of utility no building ever supplied a greater public want, while as an ornament to the town it stands unsurpassed.

The Opening Ceremony

At an early hour on Wednesday morning the sounds of the church bells pealed merrily through the air, and flags which floated from all the buildings and many of the shops in the principal streets indicated that the day was to be one of general rejoicing. The weather was all that could be desired. A number of shops were wholly and others partially closed, and some of the mills and workshops ceased working early to allow such hands as were desirous of joining in the public procession in honour of the opening an opportunity to do so. The various societies and bands of music intending to join in the procession began to form near the Borough Court at 12 o'clock.

The Market Hall by Gaslight

The Market Hall was crowded with people from soon after six o'clock to ten o'clock. It was brilliantly lit up. The Gilnow Saxhorn band occupied the platform; many people had gone there in the hope of enjoying a dance, but the building was so crowded that dancing was out of the question.

The Ball

A grand ball in celebration of the opening was held in the evening at the Baths Assembly Rooms, and was attended by the elite of the town and neighbourhood.

The first market in the hall was held on Saturday, and it being the Christmas market, there was an excellent show of all descriptions of poultry. The butchers soon disposed of their choice cuts at 7½*d* a pound. The show of Christmas geese was very meagre, but such as were in the market sold readily at 8*d* a pound.

At night the hall was so crowded that the avenues were almost impassable, and during this time several pockets were picked.

If Quite Convenient, Sir

Charles Dickens

*Before the Christmas miracle changed his life, Scrooge was a lost soul.
Here, without exaggeration or hyperbole, Dickens sums up in
remarkably few words the darkness and emptiness of his existence.*

At length the hour of shutting up the counting-house arrived. With an ill-will Scrooge dismounted from his stool, and tacitly admitted the fact to the expectant clerk in the Tank, who instantly snuffed his candle out, and put on his hat.

'You'll want all day to-morrow, I suppose?' said Scrooge.

'If quite convenient, Sir.'

'It's not convenient,' said Scrooge, 'and it's not fair. If I was to stop half-a-crown for it, you'd think yourself ill-used, I'll be bound?'

The clerk smiled faintly.

'And yet,' said Scrooge, 'you don't think me ill-used, when I pay a day's wages for no work.'

The clerk observed that it was only once a year.

'A poor excuse for picking a man's pocket every twenty-fifth of December!' said Scrooge, buttoning his great-coat to the chin. 'But I suppose you must have the whole day. Be here all the earlier next morning!'

The clerk promised he would; and Scrooge walked out with a growl. The office was closed in a twinkling, and the clerk, with the long ends of his white comforter dangling below his waist (for he boasted no great-coat), went down a slide on Cornhill, at the end of a lane of boys, twenty times, in honour of its being Christmas Eve, and then ran home to Camden Town as hard as he could pelt, to play at blindman's-buff.

Scrooge took his melancholy dinner in his usual melancholy tavern; and having read all the newspapers, and beguiled the rest of the evening with his banker's-book, went home to bed. He lived in chambers which had once belonged to his deceased partner. They were a gloomy suite of rooms, in a lowering pile of building up a yard, where it had so little business to be, that one could scarcely help fancying it must have run there when it was a young house, playing at hide-and-seek with other houses, and have forgotten the way out again. It was old enough now, and dreary enough, for nobody lived in it but Scrooge, the other rooms being all let out as offices. The yard was so dark that even Scrooge, who knew its every stone, was fain to grope with his hands. The fog and frost so hung about the black old gateway of the house, that it seemed as if the Genius of the Weather sat in mournful meditation on the threshold.

Plessy's Christmas Eve

This story from the children's magazine Little Folks *of mid-Victorian times aimed to comfort and cheer young readers who were ill over the festive period – luckless children who, given the living conditions of the time, even in middle-class homes such as the one portrayed here, must always have been around in significant numbers. It will soon be realized that the anonymous author of this piece is no Dickens, but the story is another reminder of the sentimental spirit of the age in which the master storyteller wrote, and of its emphasis on family life – even if, when it came to the choice between a Christmas Eve dinner party and staying at home with their sick daughter, it is taken for granted that the parents should choose the former.*

Plessy was ill, and it was Christmas Eve. Not so ill as to cause deep anxiety or require much attention. More was the pity! There would have been some consolation under those circumstances in not being very well. She was much too weak to get up from her little bed – too weak to trot along, as she loved to, in the clear white snow, or to join in any of the fun, which was all to take place away from home – too weak to do anything but feel the misfortune and the mistake it was to be unwell at such a season. Then her sickness made no difference to any one else: at least, although they all said they were sorry, and looked sorry, everything went on just the same as if she had been quite well.

There was Mrs Cardigan's Christmas-tree party, to which she and her brothers and sisters were always invited, going to take place just as usual; and there would be dancing and laughter and games and presents, exactly the same as there had been in the previous year, and for many years, when she was there to enjoy it all. Things didn't seem quite right to Plessy in some way. She could not understand it all, but she had a curious sort of feeling that because she was ill things ought not to go on in precisely the same manner as they did when she was well.

As she lay in her little bed under the nursery wall, she watched nurse wash and dress Mabel, and Charlie, and Harry, and little Rose, in their best evening frocks and knickerbocker suits, and listened to their joyous anticipations of the party with a curious little sense in her heart of the wrongness of everything. Nurse had constantly to subdue the happy exclamations of the rest with the reminder, 'Poor Miss Plessy is ill, and can't bear any noise.'

Then came papa's voice from the stairs, calling to nurse – 'The carriage is at the door. Aren't the little ones ready?'

'In a minute, sir,' nurse responded.

And then on Plessy's thin white cheek four pairs of soft warm lips were eagerly pressed, one after the other, and 'Good-night, Plessy; don't be asleep when we come back,' was whispered as the children hurried away.

Nurse cleared the nursery of the children's things, and set everything straight; then she turned down the lamp, so that the white glow of the snow through the uncovered windows mingled with the soft yellow light.

Plessy remembered the year before, when she was one of the happy group below – the being muffled up in soft woollen and fur wraps by mamma and papa in the hall, and lifted into the close carriage – the banging-to of the door, the 'All right!' given to Jessop, the coachman – and then the drive along the snow-covered road and up the long avenue of crystallized trees to the shining doorway of Mrs Cardigan's big house, all the windows of which were ablaze with lights.

Presently, in amongst the nursery shadows Plessy's mamma glided. She was dressed in shimmering silk, with flowers in her hair. She and papa were going out to dine at the house of another friend. She too said, 'Poor Plessy!' but in lower and more pitiful tones than nurse's.

'Don't be lonely, little one; you will sleep and get strong for to-morrow, will you not? You must be sure to be well enough for papa to carry you down to dinner, you know.'

Then came papa himself, with his good-night kiss, and injunctions to go to sleep right away, and forget that it was Christmas Eve.

Plessy bravely kept back her tears until after her parents were gone, but she could not prevent the bright drops from falling then.

Nurse brought her supper soon after: a cup of beef tea and some thin strips of dry toast, which Plessy had to swallow in spite of the lump in her throat, which kept growing bigger instead of smaller.

When the cup was empty nurse straightened her pillows, tucked her up comfortably, put a fresh lump of coal on the fire, and turned the lamp very low. Then she bent over the little bed.

'Now you'll go to sleep, little lamb, won't you?'

Plessy knew that nurse wanted to go down-stairs to supper, and that they would be merry down below, because it was Christmas Eve, and there was no one in the house to be waited upon; so she answered meekly: 'I shan't want anything else to-night, nurse; you can go now.'

'You'll be more likely to sleep if there's nobody in the room, Miss Plessy,' said nurse, and left her.

* * *

How quiet the nursery was after nurse went, with the still gleam of mingled fire and lamp-light upon the old white pictured walls! The windows were covered now, and no snow-shine came in from without. And the snow, lying thickly outside in the streets, softened the rumble of the wheels of vehicles that passed.

Plessy's papa was a doctor, and lived almost in the centre of a large town, in a comparatively quiet street. The nursery was hardly ever free from noise, except when the little white beds ranged against the walls were all filled. Now they were empty, with smooth pillows that looked as though they were waiting for each little curly head. How loudly the clock ticked over the mantelpiece! Plessy had had no idea until then how very plainly it could make itself heard. It seemed almost to be speaking with the sharp click of its pendulum, if only she could have understood its language. Even the dropping of a cinder from the grate became a matter of importance now.

For a long while Plessy watched the shadows which the fire-light cast upon the walls, tracing fanciful figures in their dim shapes. But she grew tired of this occupation, and fell to thinking about Mrs Cardigan's party of the year before, and wondering if this one would be half as nice. No other lady ever gave such nice parties as Mrs Cardigan did in the estimation of little folks; no other Christmas-tree ever came up to hers, and to miss it was to miss the one pleasure of the winter for which no other could compensate.

In the previous year a young lady, a niece of Mrs Cardigan's, had been visiting her, and she made an addition to the Christmas-tree which gave great delight, in the shape of a waxen fairy doll for its highest pinnacle. Plessy remembered how little Rose Cardigan had drawn her aside during an interval in the dances, and communicated this fact to her. From one to another the news of the fairy doll flew through the room.

Plessy recalled the thrill of anticipation which filled her own heart, and which was turned into a great longing when Rose further told her that the fairy doll was to be drawn for, and would become the absolute property of some little girl then present. Oh, if she might only be the fortunate little girl!

'Would there be a fairy of the tree this year?' Plessy asked of herself. And if so, would she be again drawn for? And who would win her? She would have no chance, and the year before it had been just as likely that the doll would fall to her as to any one else. She did not win her, but then she might have done.

The memory of the doll floated into her heart and mind now.

A Christmas Party: Rich. Illustrated London News, *25 December 1886*.

When supper was over, and the great folding doors were flung open, revealing the large Christmas-tree, blazing with innumerable tapers and laden with glittering toys, Plessy's eyes had sought the topmost spray at once for the fairy. There it was, poised upon one waxen foot by a wire.

It was a lovely wax doll with streaming flaxen hair, upon which was set a crown of gold paper with five points. Its white gauze skirts were glittering with golden tinsel; and in its outstretched waxen arms it held a golden wand with a star and crescent at one end of it. The sweet face of the doll-fairy, with its deeply-fringed blue eyes, smiled down upon the upturned faces of all the little girls of the party, each of which had on it a longing to possess it.

Plessy kept her eyes fixed upon that topmost twig of the tree. None of the toy fruit on the lower branches was to be compared for one moment with the doll.

When George Cardigan brought round the bag containing the tickets for the drawing, Plessy slipped in her little trembling hand with a great, almost irrepressible, wish swelling her heart. The tickets were made of cardboard, all cut exactly the same size, but on one of them was etched the figure of the doll, the rest all being blanks. The fortunate drawer of the etching became the possessor of the fairy from the tree.

In her nervous eagerness Plessy clutched one ticket and let it fall, then another, and drew it out. When George passed on with the silken bag to the little girl next to her, she stole a timid and furtive glance at the bit of cardboard in her hand.

The upper side was blank. With a thrill of fear she turned it over. The prize of the drawing had not fallen to her. She looked up once more to the tree. But she could not see the doll; her eyes were swimming with tears.

It had fallen to the share of little Agnes Moore, a child whose father was very rich, whose nursery was full of dolls, and who did not need this addition to them. It was a cruel thought to little Plessy that Agnes could never care for the doll as she would have done. Her papa was a hard-working doctor, and there were already five little children in his nursery, and such toys as they had to amuse them were principally of home manufacture. Her best doll had only a composition face, and nothing to speak of in the way of hair. Plessy had felt a sort of pitiful contempt for this homely doll ever since she had brought home with her from Mrs Cardigan's party the memory of the fair hair and blue eyes of the waxen fairy of the tree. And her own doll had seemed, on its part, to have had a fit of the sulks. It had never wanted to be played with since, and seemed fully to understand that its little mistress's heart had changed towards it.

* * *

Slowly the hours ticked on, and at last nurse came up. She thought Plessy was asleep, and stepped softly so as not to awaken her. From under her drooping eyelids Plessy watched her, thinking, as she saw her bright eyes, 'She has had a pleasant Christmas Eve'.

Nurse raked out the ashes from the grate, so that a little blaze sprang up and fresh shadows flickered on the walls. Then she turned down the coverlet of each little bed, and hung four little white-frilled night-dresses to the fire.

She had hardly finished these preparations when there was a sharp ring at the house door, quickly followed by the tramping of four pairs of dancing feet up the stairs, and voices talking about Plessy in no hushed tones.

Nurse rushed to the door, and Plessy heard her whispering to them to be quiet, 'and not awaken poor Miss Plessy'.

'Mabel had a box . . . which she placed on Plessy's bed.'

Plessy started upright in bed. 'I am not asleep, nurse, and I want to hear all about the party.'

In rushed four little happy figures, with tumbled hair and frocks, flushed faces and flashing eyes, and all talked at once, so that Plessy was quite bewildered.

Mabel had a box in her hands, which she placed on Plessy's bed, and all four were laden with toys, bon-bons, and trinkets. Mabel was by nature the most timid of the group, and it was some few minutes before she could make her little voice heard or attract Plessy's full attention.

'Tell me, tell me quickly!' cried Plessy, above the eager noise of the boys, who were displaying and explaining the novelty of their own Christmas-tree spoils. 'Was there a fairy doll of the tree, and who won it in the raffle?'

'A fairy!' cried Charlie. 'Of course there was; but who cares about that?'

'Please,' exclaimed Mabel, pushing the long-shaped white box into a more conspicuous position before Plessy's eyes, 'It's there; Mrs Cardigan sent it to you, Plessy.'

'I say, Pless, wasn't it jolly of her?' put in Charlie. 'She wouldn't have the doll drawn for at all, but she said there was a little girl who was ill and couldn't come to the party, and it should be sent away to her.'

'With Mrs Cardigan's kind love,' said Mabel; 'and we are to tell you how very sorry she is that you have been lonely and ill on Christmas Eve.'

'Oh!' cried Plessy, with a gasp of joy unspeakable, and her fingers fluttered with awe and trembling over the white lid, too feeble just at first, from the greatness of her surprise, to lift it.

'Come now, Master Harry; come now, Miss Mabel,' cried nurse, 'it's time you were all in bed. Why, it's close on ten o'clock, and Miss Plessy not asleep. How ever do you think she will be able to get up to-morrow?'

Mabel lingered to say to her sister, before following nurse to be undressed: 'Just look at her, Plessy! She's ever so much lovelier than the fairy doll was last year.'

Plessy drew aside the lid, and there lay the object of her dreamful longings, all glittering in white and gold, with blue fringed eyes staring up placidly into her own. Slowly she lifted it out from its bed of soft wool; slowly she examined it. It was perfect in every remembered possession, from pink face to waxen toes, from flowing hair to white gauze robes and starry wand.

'Oh, how good of Mrs Cardigan!' she exclaimed inwardly. 'But I won't forget who it was who put it into her heart to send the gift to me. Mama says all kind thoughts come from Him.'

She laid the little white doll down upon her pillow, closed her eyes and clasped her hands, while a fervent thanksgiving ascended to Him the Lord of this happy Christmas-time.

Long after the four other little tired heads were slumbering on their respective pillows, Plessy's eyes sought to assure themselves of the possession of her treasure in the dim light of the silent nursery. She had not fallen asleep when the distant sound of voices broke upon the frosty stillness of the air with the familiar carol:

Good Christian men, rejoice, rejoice!

The last sound she heard was the ringing of the bells that ushered in the Christmas morn; and, with their bright echoes in her heart, she wandered away into the land of dreams with her fairy doll of the Christmas-tree.

No Playthings

Charles Dickens

This passage from The Cricket on the Hearth *allows Dickens to return to a recurring theme – the frightening nature of children's toys. This was doubtless more true in Victorian times, when the concept of 'cute' fairies, dolls and cuddly animals was all but unknown. Even Father Christmas was a vaguely disturbing, bacchanalian figure not unlike Scrooge's Ghost of Christmas Present, or perhaps a jolly goblin – to the extent that the entirely benign and inoffensive Santa can be seen as an invention of the inter-war years of this century.*

Tackleton the Toy-merchant, pretty generally known as Gruff and Tackleton – for that was the firm, though Gruff had been bought out long ago; only leaving his name, and as some said his nature, according to its Dictionary meaning, in the business – Tackleton the Toy-merchant, was a man whose vocation had been quite misunderstood by his Parents and Guardians. If they had made him a Money Lender, or a sharp Attorney, or a Sheriff's Officer, or a Broker, he might have sown his discontented oats in his youth, and, after having had the full run of himself in ill-natured transactions, might have turned out amiable, at last, for the sake of a little freshness and novelty. But, cramped and chafing in the peaceable pursuit of toy-making, he was a domestic Ogre, who had been living on children all his life, and was their implacable enemy. He despised all toys; wouldn't have bought one for the world; delighted, in his malice, to insinuate grim expressions into the faces of brown-paper farmers who drove pigs to market, bellmen who advertised lost lawyers' consciences, moveable old ladies who darned stockings or carved pies; and other like samples of his stock in trade. In appalling masks; hideous, hairy, red-eyed Jacks in Boxes; Vampire Kites; demoniacal Tumblers who wouldn't lie down, and were perpetually flying forward, to stare infants out of countenance; his soul perfectly revelled. They were his only relief, and safety-valve.

He was great in such inventions. Anything suggestive of a Pony-nightmare, was delicious to him. He had even lost money (and he took to that toy very kindly) by getting up Goblin slides for magic-lanterns, whereon the Powers of Darkness were depicted as a sort of supernatural shell-fish, with human faces. In intensifying the

portraiture of Giants, he had sunk quite a little capital; and, though no painter himself, he could indicate, for the instruction of his artists, with a piece of chalk, a certain furtive leer for the countenances of those monsters, which was safe to destroy the peace of mind of any young gentleman between the ages of six and eleven, for the whole Christmas or Midsummer Vacation.

What he was in toys, he was (as most men are) in all other things. You may easily suppose, therefore, that within the green cape, which reached down to the calves of his legs, there was buttoned up to the chin an uncommonly pleasant fellow; and that he was about as choice a spirit, and as agreeable a companion, as ever stood in a pair of bull-headed looking boots with mahogany-coloured tops.

Games for Everybody

Phillis Browne

With Cassell's Family Magazine *in the household, there was never an excuse for a dull moment at Victorian Christmas parties.*

Some games, which are rather boisterous in their character, are known to every one and need no description. Amongst these are 'Blind Man's Buff', 'Puss in the Corner', 'Trencher', 'Blind Postman', 'Hunt the Slipper' and 'The Elements', or 'Air, Earth, Fire, and Water'. 'Proverbs', too, is a capital old game. When it is played, one member of the company leaves the room and the rest fix upon a well-known proverb. The banished guest returns, and asks each person a question, who in reply is bound to bring in one word of the proverb in its proper order, and the questioner tries to find out from these answers what the proverb is. A very amusing variety of this game is called 'Shooting Proverbs'. The guests each appropriate one word of the proverb as before. The one who is trying to guess the proverb comes in, steps into the middle of the room, and calls out in a commanding voice, 'Make ready! Present! Fire!' At the word 'Fire' all the company shout their own words at once, and the proverb is to be guessed from the sound, which is a very confusing one.

Perhaps there is no game which gives greater amusement both to young folks and old ones than the game of 'Characters', sometimes called 'Twenty Questions' and sometimes 'Nouns'. In this, one of the company thinks of some one particular person or thing, and the others ply him with questions, and endeavour to find out his secret from the answers. It is astonishing how judicious questioning can draw the most out-of-the-way object out of

SKETCHES AT WHAITE'S GERMAN FAIR.

A Manchester social magazine's impression of the city's Whaite's German Fair – 'German' because of its high quality wooden toys from that country.

mystery into the light of day. Sometimes the company divide themselves into two parties, each of which sends out one of their number, and on his return questions him separately, and endeavours to find out his secret before the other side can do so. Each candidate must be questioned by the opposite side, and the party which first guesses rightly takes possession of both candidates. That side is considered to have won the game which draws over the largest number of members. When played in this way, this game is often called 'Clumps'.

'Russian Scandal' is a very interesting game. In this game one member of the company writes a short story on a slate, making it as full of incident as he can. He then goes outside the door, and calls one of his companions to him and reads the story aloud once, very distinctly. After doing this, he walks away and carries the slate with him. The person to whom the story was read summons another of the party, and narrates the story to him as exactly as he can remember it. The third person tells it to a fourth, and the fourth to a fifth, and so on till each one of the party has had the story narrated to him privately and solemnly outside the door.

When all have heard it, the last one to go out comes into the room and narrates the story to the whole company. The original is then read from the slate, and it is quite curious to notice how it has altered in the course of transmission. There is no necessity for any intentional inaccuracy. If only there is plenty of incident in the tale, it will be found that it is almost impossible for the person who last heard the story to repeat it exactly as the first one gave it. The little fuss that is made in entering and leaving the room makes the difficulty of remembrance all the greater.

Good to be Children

Charles Dickens

Scrooge and the Ghost of Christmas Present look in on a party at his merry nephew's house – and discover typically flirtatious Victorian goings-on.

After a while they played at forfeits; for it is good to be children sometimes, and never better than at Christmas, when its mighty Founder was a child himself. Stop! There was first a game at blind-man's buff. Of course there was. And I no more believe Topper was really blind than I believe he had eyes in his boots. My opinion is, that it was a done thing between him and Scrooge's nephew: and that the Ghost of Christmas Present knew it. The way he went after that plump sister in the lace tucker, was an outrage on the credulity of human nature. Knocking down the fire-irons, tumbling over the chairs, bumping up against the piano, smothering himself among the curtains, wherever she went, there went he. He always knew where the plump sister was. He wouldn't catch anybody else. If you had fallen up against him, as some of them did, and stood there; he would have made a feint of endeavouring to seize you, which would have been an affront to your understanding; and would instantly have sidled off in the direction of the plump sister. She often cried out that it wasn't fair; and it really was not. But when at last, he caught her; when, in spite of all her silken rustlings, and her rapid flutterings past him, he got her into a corner whence there was no escape; then his conduct was the most execrable. For his pretending not to know her; his pretending that it was necessary to touch her head-dress, and further to assure himself of her identity by pressing a

certain ring upon her finger, and a certain chain about her neck; was vile, monstrous! No doubt she told him her opinion of it, when, another blind man being in office, they were so very confidential together, behind the curtains.

Terrible Tumbler

Charles Dickens

This piece comes from a famous essay, 'A Christmas Tree', published in Household Words *on Saturday 21 December 1850. Again it tells of the author's almost morbid fascination with grotesque toys.*

Straight, in the middle of the room, cramped in the freedom of its growth by no encircling walls or soon-reached ceiling, a shadowy tree arises; and, looking up into the dreamy brightness of its top – for I observe, in this tree, the singular property that it appears to grow downward towards the earth – I look into my youngest Christmas recollections!

All toys at first, I find. Up yonder, among the green holly and red berries, is the Tumbler with his hands in his pockets, who wouldn't lie down, but whenever he was put upon the floor, persisted in rolling his fat body about, until he rolled himself still, and brought those lobster eyes of his to bear upon me – when I affected to laugh very much, but in my heart of hearts was extremely doubtful of him. Close beside him is that infernal snuff-box, out of which there sprang a demoniacal Counsellor in a black gown, with an obnoxious head of hair, and a red cloth mouth, wide open, who was not to be endured on any terms, but could not be put away either; for he used suddenly, in a highly magnified state, to fly out of Mammoth Snuff-boxes in dreams, when least expected. Nor is the frog with cobbler's wax on his tail, far off; for there was no knowing where he wouldn't jump; and when he flew over the candle, and came upon one's hand with that spotted back – red on a green ground – he was horrible. The cardboard lady in a blue-silk skirt, who was stood up against the candlestick to dance, and whom I see on the same branch, was milder, and was beautiful; but I can't say as much for the larger cardboard man, who used to be hung against the wall and pulled by a string; there was a sinister expression in that nose of

his; and when he got his legs round his neck (which he very often did), he was ghastly, and not a creature to be alone with.

When did that dreadful Mask first look at me? Who put it on, and why was I so frightened that the sight of it is an era in my life? It is not a hideous visage in itself; it is even meant to be droll; why then were its stolid features so intolerable? Surely not because it hid the wearer's face. An apron would have done as much; and though I should have preferred even the apron away, would it not have been absolutely insupportable, like the mask? Was it the immovability of the mask? The doll's face was immovable, but I was not afraid of her. Perhaps that fixed and set change coming over a real face, infused into my quickened heart some remote suggestion and dread of the universal change that is to come on every face, and make it still? Nothing reconciled me to it.

No drummers, from whom proceeded a melancholy chirping on the turning of a handle; no regiment of soldiers, with a mute band, taken out of a box, and fitted, one by one, upon a stiff and lazy little set of lazy-tongs; no old woman, made of wires and a brown-paper composition, cutting up a pie for two small children, could give me permanent comfort, for a long time. Nor was it any satisfaction to be shown the Mask, and see that it was made of paper, or to have it locked up and be assured that no one wore it. The mere recollection of that fixed face, the mere knowledge of its existence anywhere, was sufficient to awake me in the night all perspiration and horror, with 'O I know it's coming! O the mask!'

Disastrous Week

M a r y   R u s s e l l   M i t f o r d

This excerpt from Our Village, *published in 1848, fully supports the author's claim that she was making 'an attempt to delineate country scenery and country manners, as they exist in a small village in the south of England . . . Descriptions . . . written on the spot, and at the moment, and in nearly every instance with the closest and most resolute fidelity to the places and the people.' Here she tells of the landlady of the village inn, Hester Frost, preparing for a Christmas party.*

Of the unrest of that week of bustling preparation, words can give but a faint image – Oh, the scourings, the cleanings, the sandings, the dustings, the scoldings of that disastrous week! The lame ostler and the red-haired parish girl were worked off their feet – 'even Sunday shone no Sabbath-day to them' – for then did the lame ostler trudge eight miles to the church of a neighbouring parish, to procure the attendance of a celebrated bassoon player to officiate in lieu of Timothy; whilst the poor little maid was sent nearly as far to the next town, in quest of an itinerant show-woman, of whom report had spoken at the Bell, to beat the tambourine. The show-woman proved undiscoverable; but the bassoon player having promised to come, and to bring with him a clarionet, Mrs Frost was at ease as to her music; and having provided more victuals than the whole village could have discussed at a sitting, and having moreover adorned her house with berried holly, china-roses, and chrysanthemums, after the most tasteful manner, began to enter into the spirit of the thing, and to wish for the return of her husband, to admire and to praise.

Late on the great day Jacob arrived, his cart laden with marine stores for his share of the festival. Never had our goodly village witnessed such a display of oysters, mussels, periwinkles, and cockles, to say nothing of apples and nuts, and

two little kegs, snugly covered up, which looked exceedingly as if they had cheated the revenue, a packet of green tea, which had something of the same air, and a new silk gown, of a flaming salmon-colour, straight from Paris, which he insisted on Hester's retiring to assume, whilst he remained to arrange the table and receive the company, who, it being now about four o'clock pm – our good rustics can never have enough of a good thing – were beginning to assemble for the ball.

The afternoon was fair and cold, and dry and frosty, and Matthewses, Bridgwaters, Whites, and Joneses, in short the whole farmerage and shopkeepery of the place, with a goodly proportion of wives and daughters, came pouring in apace. Jacob received them with much gallantry, uncloaking and unbonneting the ladies, assisted by his two staring and awkward auxiliaries, welcoming their husbands and fathers, and apologizing, as best he might, for the absence of his helpmate; who, 'perplexed in the extreme' by her new finery, which happening to button down the back, she was fain to put on hind side before, did not make her appearance till the greater part of the company had arrived, and the music had struck up a country dance. An evil moment, alas! did poor Hester choose for her entry! For the first sound that met her ear was Timothy's fiddle, forming a strange trio with the bassoon and the clarionet: and the first persons whom she saw were Tom Higgs cracking walnuts at the chimney-side, and Sandy Frazer saluting the widow Glen under the mistletoe. How she survived such sights and sounds does appear wonderful – but survive them she did – for at three o'clock am, when our reporter left the party, she was engaged in a social game at cards, which, by the description, seems to have been long whist, with the identical widow Glen, Sandy Frazer, and William Ford, and had actually won fivepence-halfpenny of Martha's money; the young folks were still dancing gaily, to the sound of Timothy's fiddle, which fiddle had the good quality of going on almost as well drunk as sober, and it was now playing solo, the clarionet being *hors-de-combat* and the bassoon under the table. Tom Higgs, after showing off more tricks than a monkey, amongst the rest sewing the whole card-party together by the skirts, to the probable damage of Mrs Frost's gay gown, had returned to his old post by the fire, and his old amusement of cracking walnuts, with the shells of which he was pelting the little parish girl, who sat fast asleep on the other side; and Jacob Frost in all his glory, sat in a cloud of tobacco smoke, roaring out catches with his old friend George Bridgwater, and half a dozen other 'drowthy cronies', whilst 'aye the ale was growing better', and the Christmas party went merrily on.

Christmas Eve Mystery

Charles Dickens

*Perhaps the most dramatic Christmas event of all in Dickens' work is
the murder of Edwin Drood. The happy occasion only serves to
emphasize the horror of the deed in this, the last of the master's novels.*

Christmas Eve in Cloisterham. A few strange faces in the streets; a few
other faces, half strange and half familiar, once the faces of Cloisterham
children, now the faces of men and women who come back from the outer
world at long intervals to find the city wonderfully shrunken in size, as if it
had not washed by any means well in the meanwhile. To these, the striking
of the Cathedral clock, and the cawing of the rooks from the Cathedral
tower, are like voices of their nursery time. To such as these, it has happened
in their dying hours afar off, that they have imagined their chamber floor to
be strewn with the autumnal leaves fallen from the elm trees in the Close: so
have the rustling sounds and fresh scents of their earliest impressions revived
when the circle of their lives was very nearly traced, and the beginning and
the end were drawing close together.

Seasonable tokens are about. Red berries shine here and there in the
lattices of Minor Canon Corner; Mr and Mrs Tope are daintily sticking
sprigs of holly into the carvings and sconces of the Cathedral stalls, as if
they were sticking them into the coat-buttonholes of the Dean and Chapter.
Lavish profusion is in the shops: particularly in the articles of currants,
raisins, spices, candied peel, and moist sugar. An unusual air of gallantry
and dissipation is abroad; evinced in an immense bunch of mistletoe
hanging in the greengrocer's shop doorway, and a poor little Twelfth Cake,
culminating in the figure of a Harlequin – such a very poor little Twelfth
Cake, that one would rather call it a Twenty-Fourth Cake, or a Forty-Eighth
Cake – to be raffled for at the pastry-cook's, terms one shilling per member.
Public amusements are not wanting. The Wax-Work which made so deep an
impression on the reflective mind of the Emperor of China is to be seen by
particular desire during Christmas Week only, on the premises of the
bankrupt livery-stable keeper up the lane; and a new grand comic Christmas

pantomime is to be produced at the Theatre: the latter heralded by the portrait of Signor Jacksonini the clown, saying 'How do you do to-morrow?' quite as large as life, and almost as miserably. In short, Cloisterham is up and doing: though from this description the High School and Miss Twinkleton's are to be excluded. From the former establishment, the scholars have gone home, every one of them in love with one of Miss Twinkleton's young ladies (who knows nothing about); and only the handmaidens flutter occasionally in the windows of the latter. It is noticed, by-and-bye, that these damsels become, within the limits of decorum, more skittish when thus entrusted with the concrete representation of their sex, than when dividing the representation with Miss Twinkleton's young ladies.

* * *

All through the night the wind blows, and abates not. But early in the morning, when there is barely enough light in the east to dim the stars, it begins to lull. From that time, with occasional wild charges, like a wounded monster dying, it drops and sinks; and at full daylight it is dead.

It is then seen that the hands of the Cathedral clock are torn off; that lead from the roof has been stripped away, rolled up, and blown into the Close; and that some stones have been displaced upon the summit of the great tower. Christmas morning though it be, it is necessary to send up workmen, to ascertain the extent of the damage done. These, led by Durdles, go aloft; while Mr Tope and a crowd of early idlers gather down in Minor Canon Corner, shading their eyes and watching for their appearance up there.

This cluster is suddenly broken and put aside by the hands of Mr Jasper; all the gazing eyes are brought down to the earth by his loudly enquiring of Mr Crisparkle, at an open window:

'Where is my nephew?'

'He has not been here. Is he not with you?'

'No. He went down to the river last night, with Mr Neville, to look at the storm, and has not been back. Call Mr Neville!'

'He left this morning, early.'

'Left this morning, early? Let me in, let me in!'

There is no more looking up at the tower, now. All the assembled eyes are turned on Mr Jasper, white, half-dressed, panting, and clinging to the rail before the Minor Canon's house.

Neville Landless had started so early and walked at so good a pace, that when the church bells began to ring in Cloisterham for morning service, he was eight miles away. As he wanted his breakfast by that time, having set forth on a crust of bread, he stopped at the next road-side tavern to refresh.

Visitors in want of breakfast – unless they were horses or cattle, for which class of guests there was preparation enough in the way of water-trough and hay – were so unusual at the sign of The Tilted Wagon, that it took a long time to get the wagon into the track of tea and toast and bacon. Neville, in the interval, sitting in a sanded parlour, wondering in how long time after he had gone, the sneezy fire of damp faggots would begin to make somebody else warm.

Indeed, The Tilted Wagon, as a cool establishment on the top of a hill, where the ground before the door was puddled with damp hoofs and trodden straw; where a scolding landlady slapped a moist baby (with one red sock on and one wanting) in the bar; where the cheese was cast aground upon a shelf, in company with a mouldy tablecloth and a green-handled knife, in a sort of cast-iron canoe; where the pale-faced bread shed tears of crumb over its shipwreck in another canoe; where the family linen, half washed and half dried, led a public life of lying about; where everything to drink was drunk out of mugs, and everything else was suggestive of a rhyme to mugs; The Tilted Wagon, all these things considered, hardly kept its painted promise of providing good entertainment for Man and Beast. However, Man, in the present case, was not critical, but took what entertainment he could get, and went on again after a longer rest than he needed.

He stopped at some quarter of a mile from the house, hesitating whether to pursue the road, or to follow a cart-track between two high hedgerows, which led across the slope of a breezy heath, and evidently struck into the road again by-and-bye. He decided in favour of this latter track, and pursued it with some toil; the rise being steep, and the way worn into deep ruts.

He was labouring along, when he became aware of some other pedestrians behind him. As they were coming up a faster pace than his, he stood aside, against one of the high banks, to let them pass. But their manner was very curious. Only four of them passed. Other four slackened speed, and loitered as intending to follow him when he should go on. The remainder of the party (half a dozen perhaps) turned, and went back at a great rate.

He looked at the four behind him, and he looked at the four before him. They all returned his look. He resumed his way. The four in advance went on, constantly looking back; the four in the rear came closing up.

When they all ranged out from the narrow track upon the open slope of the heath, and this order was maintained, let him diverge as he would to either side, there was no longer room to doubt that he was beset by these fellows. He stopped, as a last test; and they all stopped.

'Why do you attend upon me in this way?' he asked the whole body. 'Are you a pack of thieves?'

'Don't answer him,' said one of the number; he did not see which. 'Better be quiet.'

'Better be quiet?' repeated Neville. 'Who said so?'

Nobody replied.

'It's good advice, whichever of you skulkers gave it,' he went on angrily. 'I will not submit to be penned in between four men there, and four men there. I wish to pass, and I mean to pass, those four in front.'

They were all standing still: himself included.

'If eight men, or four men, or two men, set upon one,' he proceeded, growing more enraged, 'the one has no choice but to set his mark upon some of them. And by the Lord I'll do it, if I am interrupted any further!'

Shouldering his heavy stick, and quickening his pace, he shot on to pass the four ahead. The largest and strongest man of the number changed swiftly to the side on which he came up, and dexterously closed with him and went down with him; but not before the heavy stick had descended smartly.

'Let him be!' said this man in a suppressed voice, as they struggled together on the grass. 'Fair play! His is the build of a girl to mine, and he's got a weight strapped to his back besides. Let him alone. I'll manage him.'

After a little rolling about, in a close scuffle which caused the faces of both to be besmeared with blood, the man took his knee from Neville's chest, and rose, saying: 'There! Now take him arm-in-arm, any two of you!'

It was immediately done.

'As to our being a pack of thieves, Mr Landless,' said the man, as he spat out some blood, and wiped more from his face: 'you know better than that, at midday. We wouldn't have touched you, if you hadn't forced us. We're going to take you round to the high road, anyhow, and you'll find help enough against thieves there, if you want it. Wipe his face somebody; see how it's a-trickling down him!'

When his face was cleansed, Neville recognized in the speaker, Joe, driver of the Cloisterham omnibus, whom he had seen but once, and that on the day of his arrival.

'And what I recommend you for the present, is, don't talk, Mr Landless. You'll find a friend waiting for you, at the high road – gone ahead by the other way when we split into two parties – and you had much better say nothing till you come up with him. Bring that stick along, somebody else, and let's be moving!'

Utterly bewildered, Neville stared around him and said not a word. Walking between his two conductors, who held his arms in theirs, he went on, as in a dream: until they came again into the high road, and into the midst of a little group of people. The men who had turned back were among the group and its central figures were Mr Jasper and Mr Crisparkle. Neville's conductors took him up to the Minor Canon, and there released him, as an act of deference to that gentleman.

'What is all this, sir? What is the matter? I feel as if I had lost my senses!' cried Neville, the group closing in around him.

'Where is my nephew?' asked Mr Jasper, wildly.

'Where is your nephew?' repeated Neville. 'Why do you ask me?'

'I ask you,' retorted Jasper, 'because you were the last person in his company, and he is not to be found.'

'Not to be found!' cried Neville, aghast.

'Stay, stay,' said Mr Crisparkle. 'Permit me, Jasper. Mr Neville, you are confounded; collect your thoughts; it is of great importance that you should collect your thoughts; attend to me.'

'I will try, sir, but I seem mad.'

'You left Mr Jasper's last night, with Edwin Drood?'

'Yes.'

'At what hour?'

'Was it at twelve o'clock?' asked Neville, with his hand to his confused head, and appealing to Jasper.

'Quite right,' said Mr Crisparkle; 'the hour Mr Jasper has already named to me. You went down to the river together.'

'Undoubtedly. To see the action of the wind there.'

'What followed? How long did you stay there?'

'About ten minutes; I should say not more. We then walked together to your house, and he took leave of me at the door.'

'Did he say that he was going down to the river again?'

'No. He said that he was going straight back.'

The bystanders looked at one another, and at Mr Crisparkle. To whom Mr Jasper, who had been intensely watching Neville, said, in a low distinct suspicious voice: 'What are those stains upon his dress?'

All eyes were turned towards the blood upon his clothes.

'And here are the same stains upon this stick!' said Jasper taking it from the hand of the man who held it. 'I know the stick to be his, and he carried it last night. What does this mean?'

'In the name of God, say what it means, Neville!' urged Mr Crisparkle.

'That man and I,' said Neville, pointing out his late adversary, 'had a struggle for the stick just now, and you may see the same marks on him, sir. What was I to suppose, when I found myself molested by eight people? Could I dream of the true reason when they would give me none at all?'

Christmas with the Queen

Prince Albert died in 1861, after which Queen Victoria tended to retreat to a strictly country house style of Christmas at Osborne House on the Isle of Wight, rewarding the estate workers in the time-honoured fashion. This magazine article of mid-Victorian times gives a somewhat breathless account of what went on . . .

This afternoon a pleasant little festivity has been celebrated at Osborne House, where Her Majesty, with an ever-kindly interest in her servants and dependants, has for many years inaugurated Christmas in a similar way, the children of her tenantry and the old and infirm enjoying by the Royal bounty the first taste of Christmas fare. The Osborne estate now comprises 5,000 acres, and it includes the Prince Consort's model farm. The children of the labourers – who are housed in excellent cottages – attend the Whippingham National Schools, a pretty block of buildings,

distant one mile from Osborne. About half the number of scholars live upon the Queen's estate, and, in accordance with annual custom, the mistresses of the schools, the Misses Thomas, accompanied by the staff of teachers, have conducted a little band of boys and girls – fifty-four in all – to the house, there to take tea and to receive the customary Christmas gifts.

Until very recently the Queen herself presided at the distribution; but the Princess Beatrice has lately relieved her mother of the fatigue involved; for the ceremony is no mere formality, it is made the occasion of many a kindly word the remembrance of which far outlasts the gifts. All sorts of rumours are current on the estate for weeks before this Christmas Eve gathering as to the nature of the presents to be bestowed, for no one is supposed to know beforehand what they will be; but there was a pretty shrewd guess to-day that the boys would be given gloves, and the girls cloaks. In some cases the former had had scarves or cloth for suits, and the latter dresses, or shawls. Whatever the Christmas presents may be, here they are, arranged upon tables in two long lines, in the servants' hall. To this holly-decorated apartment the expectant youngsters are brought, and their delighted gaze falls upon a huge Christmas-tree laden with beautiful toys. Everybody knows that the tree will be there, and moreover that its summit will be crowned with a splendid doll. Now, the ultimate ownership of this doll is a matter of much concern; it needs deliberation, as it is awarded to the best child, and the judges are the children themselves. The trophy is handed to the keeping of Miss Thomas, and on the next 1st of May the children select by their votes the most popular girl in the school to be elected May Queen. To her the gift goes, and no fairer way could be devised. The Princess Beatrice always makes a point of knowing to whom the prize has been awarded. Her Royal Highness is so constantly a visitor to the cottagers and to the school that she has many an inquiry to make of the little ones as they come forward to receive their gifts.

The girls are called up first by the mistress, and Mr Andrew Blake, the steward, introduces each child to the Princess Beatrice, to whom Mr Blake hands the presents that her Royal Highness may bestow them upon the recipients with a word of good will, which makes the day memorable. Then the boys are summoned to participate in the distribution of good things, which, it should be explained, consist not only of seasonable and sensible clothing, but toys from the tree, presented by the Queen's grandchildren, who, with their parents, grace the ceremony with their presence and make the occasion one of family interest. The Ladies-in-Waiting also attend. Each boy and girl gets in addition a nicely-bound story-book and a large slice of plum pudding neatly packed in paper, and if any little one is sick at home its portion is carefully reserved.

But the hospitality of the Queen is not limited to the children. On alternate years the old men and women resident on the estate are given, under the same pleasant auspices, presents of blankets or clothing. To-day it was the turn of the men, and they received tweed for suits. The aged people have their pudding as well. For the farm labourers and boys, who are not bidden to this entertainment, there is a distribution of tickets, each representing a goodly joint of beef for the Christmas dinner. The festivity this afternoon was brought to a close by the children singing the National Anthem in the courtyard.

Never Such a Goose

Charles Dickens

*A Christmas Carol gave us so many memorable moments and
unforgettable phrases – and no passage more than this one, with its
hymn of praise for the Cratchits' humble but happy meal and the
legendary contribution to the festivities of Tiny Tim.*

Such a bustle ensued that you might have thought a goose the rarest
of all birds; a feathered phenomenon, to which a black swan was a
matter of course – and in truth it was something very like it in that
house. Mrs Cratchit made the gravy (ready beforehand in a little
saucepan) hissing hot; Master Peter mashed the potatoes with
incredible vigour; Miss Belinda sweetened up the apple-sauce; Martha
dusted the hot plates; Bob took
Tiny Tim beside him in a tiny
corner at the table; the two young
Cratchits set chairs for everybody,
not forgetting themselves, and
mounting guard upon their posts,
crammed spoons into their
mouths, lest they should shriek for
goose before their turn came to be
helped.

Scrooge's third visitor.

At last the dishes were set on, and
grace was said. It was succeeded by a
breathless pause, as Mrs Cratchit,
looking slowly all along the carving-
knife, prepared to plunge it in the
breast; but when she did, and when
the long expected gush of stuffing
issued forth, one murmur of delight
arose all round the board, and even
Tiny Tim, excited by the two young

Cratchits, beat on the table with the handle of his knife, and feebly cried Hurrah!

There never was such a goose. Bob said he didn't believe there ever was such a goose cooked. Its tenderness and flavour, size and cheapness, were the themes of universal admiration. Eked out by apple-sauce and mashed potatoes, it was sufficient dinner for the whole family; indeed, as Mrs Cratchit said with great delight (surveying one small atom of a bone upon the dish), they hadn't ate it all at last! Yet every one had had enough, and the youngest Cratchits in particular, were steeped in sage and onion to the eyebrows! But now, the plates being changed by Miss Belinda, Mrs Cratchit left the room alone – too nervous to bear witnesses – to take the pudding up and bring it in.

Suppose it should not be done enough! Suppose it should break in turning out! Suppose somebody should have got over the wall of the back-yard, and stolen it, while they were merry with the goose – a supposition at which the two young Cratchits became livid! All sorts of horrors were supposed.

Hallo! A great deal of steam! The pudding was out of the copper. A smell like a washing-day! That was the cloth. A smell like an eating-house and a pastrycook's next door to each other, with a laundress's next door to that! That was the pudding! In half a minute Mrs Cratchit entered – flushed, but smiling proudly – with the pudding, like a speckled cannon-ball, so hard and firm, blazing in half of half-a-quartern of ignited brandy, and bedight with Christmas holly stuck into the top.

Oh, a wonderful pudding! Bob Cratchit said, and calmly too, that he regarded it as the greatest success achieved by Mrs Cratchit since their marriage. Mrs Cratchit said that now the weight was off her mind, she would confess she had had her doubts about the quantity of flour. Everybody had something to say about it, but nobody said or thought it was at all a small pudding for a large family. It would have been flat heresy to do so. Any Cratchit would have blushed to hint at such a thing.

At last the dinner was all done, the cloth was cleared, the hearth swept, and the fire made up. The compound in the jug being tasted, and considered perfect, apples and oranges were put upon the table, and a shovel-full of chestnuts on the fire. Then all the Cratchit family drew round the hearth, in what Bob Cratchit called a circle, meaning half a one; and at Bob Cratchit's elbow stood the family display of glass. Two tumblers, and a custard-cup without a handle.

These held the hot stuff from the jug, however, as well as golden goblets would have done; and Bob served it out with beaming looks, while the chestnuts on the fire sputtered and cracked noisily. Then Bob proposed:

'A Merry Christmas to us all, my dears. God bless us!'

Which all the family re-echoed.

'God bless us every one!' said Tiny Tim, the last of all.

The Christmas Goose

William McGonagall

William McGonagall, born in Scotland in 1830, is rightly famous for his awful poetry. What this verse makes clear is that his feelings were not of the finest, either. Much has been made in this book of the Victorians' sense of obligation to the poor, especially at Christmas. Evidently this son of a handloom weaver had no such liberal hang-ups. It is hard to believe that the goose and the juvenile thief were not directly inspired by Dickens. Unhappily, the master's message of goodwill to all men seems to have been lost somewhere along the way . . .

> Mr Smiggs was a gentleman,
> And lived in London town;
> His wife she was a good kind soul,
> And seldom known to frown.
>
> 'Twas on Christmas eve,
> And Smiggs and his wife lay cosy in bed,
> When the thought of buying a goose
> Came into his head.
>
> So the next morning,
> Just as the sun rose,
> He jump'd out of bed,
> And he donn'd his clothes.

Saying, 'Peggy, my dear,
You need not frown,
For I'll buy you the best goose
In all London town.'

So away to the poultry shop he goes,
And bought the goose, as he did propose,
And for it he paid one crown,
The finest, he thought, in London town.

When Smiggs bought the goose
He suspected no harm,
But a naughty boy stole it
From under his arm.

Then Smiggs he cried, 'Stop, thief!
Come back with my goose!'
But the naughty boy laughed at him,
And gave him much abuse.

But a policeman captur'd the naughty boy,
And gave the goose to Smiggs,
And said he was greatly bother'd
By a set of juvenile prigs.

So the naughty boy was put in prison
For stealing the goose,
And got ten days' confinement
Before he got loose.

So Smiggs ran home to his dear Peggy,
Saying, 'Hurry, and get this fat goose ready,
That I have bought for one crown;
So, my darling, you need not frown.'

'Dear Mr Smiggs, I will not frown:
I'm sure 'tis cheap for one crown,

Especially at Christmas time –
Oh! Mr Smiggs, it's really fine.'

'Peggy, it is Christmas time,
So let us drive dull care away,
For we have got a Christmas goose,
So cook it well, I pray.

'No matter how the poor are clothed,
Or if they starve at home,
We'll drink our wine, and eat our goose,
Aye, and pick it to the bone.'

Singers from Afar

Charles Rose

This recollection of Charles Rose, a draper from Dorking in Surrey, who was born in 1818 and died in 1879, was published in book form in 1878. Looking back to a time ranging from the days of George IV to the earliest years of Victoria's reign, it tells of the kind of Christmas of Dickens' youth, before all the influences of the middle years of the century made their mark. The last line of the excerpt suggests that the link between smoking and painful, life-threatening illness was known to the man in the street at least 120 years ago; but as they say, there's none so blind . . .

The Festival of Christmas, it is needless to remark, was generally observed in Dorking half a century ago, although as was the case with other old anniversaries, differently in some respects from the way it is now. Then, as at the present time, the approach of the festive season was indicated by fine exhibitions of beef and other meat in the butchers' shops, by shows of geese and capons at the poulterers, and by piles of pudding and dessert fruits, decorated with holly, in the grocers' windows.

The Dorking Town Band, which at that time favourably compared with the bands of the neighbouring places, heralded the season by playing for some nights previous to Christmas in front of the residences of the principal inhabitants. Then, too, were heard the waits, the most famous of whom were the Ditchling Singers, who came from their distant home in Sussex to sing the carols of Christmas. The leader of these celebrated songsters was the clerk at the Ditchling Parish Church, where even at the present day the musical part of the service is simply vocal, and where may be seen that now almost obsolete instrument, the old wooden pitch pipe – probably the very same that

was used when the old clerk and his fellow choristers visited the towns of Sussex and Surrey fifty years ago.

Christmas carols in those bygone years were highly popular, and sheets of them, illustrated by wood cuts, quaint in design and rude in execution, were eagerly purchased. These productions were no doubt written by well-meaning persons, but some of them, it must be admitted, were anything but commendable.

Christmas Eve was a time of great merriment and activity – and, I am sorry to add, of no little intemperance. Then the elder wine cask was tapped, and this favourite beverage, made hot, was freely supplied to calling friends and neighbours, and to the customers generally of the trading establishments. The coaches which in the morning and on previous days had carried to London Christmas boxes of game and poultry for cockney friends, now brought down distant-dwelling natives, and baskets of cod fish and barrels of oysters for country cousins or country customers. In fact at this time Christmas presents everywhere abounded, and the poor and needy were by no means forgotten. Then as now, at the mansions of some of the neighbouring gentry, the Christmas bullock was liberally distributed.

Christmas Day was ushered in by the ringing of the church bells and the strains of the band. The tunes of the latter were usually of a sacred character, but I remember the band playing on one or two Christmas mornings, forty or five-and-forty years ago, the tune 'Get up! Get up! And Put the Pudding in the Pot', a reminder which some of the housewives of the period, drowsy from overwork, probably needed. Whatever some may have thought of this secular tune, it was certainly in unison with the festive aspect of the season, and not more inappropriate in other respects than the air 'The Girl I Left Behind Me', played by the juvenile fife and drum band on Christmas mornings of recent years.

On Christmas Day there was divine service both morning and afternoon at the Parish Church, the decorations of the building being of the simplest character. There was usually no service at the Independent place of worship, some of the congregation of the latter tending to attend the Sunday evening services of the former. The shops of the members of the Society of Friends, as on Good Friday, were kept open throughout the day, and their Meeting House, unless Christmas Day fell on their usual day of meeting, was uniformly closed.

The general fare of all classes on Christmas Day was the roast beef of Old England and the proverbial plum pudding; and around the Christmas dinner table was then, as at present, the happy place of family gatherings – although, as in some instances now, the vacant chair would call up cherished memories of departed loved ones.

The day after Christmas in bygone years was not, as at present, a general holiday. The trading establishments were all open, and their assistants, with few exceptions, at work. To the Christmas boxers it was otherwise, for the day to them was a high day and holiday. Then there were not only specially kind inquiries after the health of the household by the postman, the milkman, the waterman, the butcher, the baker, the chimney sweep and by apprentices generally, but polite calls from, and wishes of, 'A Merry Christmas and a Happy New Year' by bricklayers, carpenters, plumbers and painters, blacksmiths, whitesmiths, wheelwrights, and I almost forget who else besides.

Christmas merry-making and a generous hospitality everywhere prevailed, and social parties were abundantly plentiful. The usual music at such parties then was not that now popular instrument the piano, but the violin, or as it was then generally called, the fiddle. At that time, indeed, it was thought to be quite consistent with the social status of the trading and even of the professional classes to engage for a party, or simply for the gratification of the household, the services of the humble fiddler and pipe and tabor player.

Two of the most popular of these unpretending musicians were fiddler Charley Cleere and piper Hilton, who played such airs as 'Auld Lang Syne', 'Home, Sweet Home', 'In a Cottage near a Wood', 'The Merry Swiss Boy' and other old-fashioned tunes. For the fiddler and his companion would be reserved some of the best elder wine and perhaps a piece of the Christmas pudding or a mince or Christmas pie to ensure 'a happy month in the New Year'. What became of piper Hilton I know not, but poor old Charley's fiddling career was, I well remember, brought to an end by a painful malady caused, it was said, by the 'weed' he loved so well.

Yo ho, there! Ebenezer!

Charles Dickens

The Ghost of Christmas Past shows Scrooge the old times, when he was apprenticed to the fun-loving Fezziwig. This sophisticated piece of writing, from a novelist in his early twenties, does not overstate the young Scrooge's jollity. He enters into the spirit of his master's party well enough, but there is nothing here that makes it inconceivable that he should grow up into a bitter, misanthropic man.

Old Fezziwig laid down his pen, and looked up at the clock, which pointed to the hour of seven. He rubbed his hands; adjusted his capacious waistcoat; laughed all over himself, from his shoes to his organ of benevolence; and called out in a comfortable, oily, rich, fat, jovial voice:

'Yo ho, there! Ebenezer! Dick!'

Scrooge's former self, now grown a young man, came briskly in, accompanied by his fellow-'prentice.

'Dick Wilkins, to be sure!' said Scrooge to the Ghost. 'Bless me, yes. There he is. He was very much attached to me, was Dick. Poor Dick! Dear, dear!'

'Yo ho, my boys!' said Fezziwig. 'No more work to-night. Christmas Eve, Dick. Christmas, Ebenezer! Let's have the shutters up,' cried old Fezziwig, with a sharp clap of his hands, 'before a man can say Jack Robinson!'

You wouldn't believe how those two fellows went at it! They charged into the street with the shutters – one, two, three – had 'em up in their places – four, five, six – barred 'em and pinned 'em – seven, eight, nine – and came back before you could have got to twelve, panting like race-horses.

'Hilli-ho!' cried old Fezziwig, skipping down from the high desk, with wonderful agility. 'Clear away, my lads, and let's have lots of room here! Hilli-ho, Dick! Chirrup, Ebenezer!'

Clear away! There was nothing they wouldn't have cleared away, or couldn't have cleared away, with old Fezziwig looking on. It was done in a minute. Every movable was packed off, as if it were dismissed from public life for evermore; the floor was swept and watered, the lamps were trimmed, fuel was heaped upon the fire; and the warehouse was as snug, and warm, and dry, and bright a ball-room, as you would desire to see upon a winter's night.

In came a fiddler with a music-book, and went up to the lofty desk, and made an orchestra of it, and tuned like fifty stomach-aches. In came Mrs Fezziwig, one vast substantial smile. In came the three Miss Fezziwigs, beaming and lovable. In came the six young followers whose hearts they broke. In came all the young men and women employed in the business. In came the housemaid, with her cousin, the baker. In came the cook, with her brother's particular friend, the milkman. In came the boy from over the way, who was suspected of not having board enough from his master; trying to hide himself behind the girl from next door but one, who was proved to have had her ears pulled by her mistress. In they all came, one after another; some shyly, some boldly, some gracefully, some awkwardly, some pushing, some pulling; in they all came, anyhow and everyhow. Away they all went, twenty couple at once, hands half round and back again the other way; down the middle and up again; round and round in various stages of affectionate grouping; old top couple always turning up in the wrong place; new top couple starting off again, as soon as they got there; all top couples at last, and not a bottom one to help them. When this result was brought about, old Fezziwig, clapping his hands to stop the dance, cried out, 'Well done!' and the fiddler plunged his hot face into a pot of porter, especially provided for that purpose. But scorning rest upon his reappearance, he instantly began again, though there were no dancers yet, as if the other fiddler had been carried home, exhausted, on a shutter; and he were a brand-new man resolved to beat him out of sight, or perish.

There were more dances, and there were forfeits, and more dances, and there was cake, and there was negus, and there was a great piece of Cold Roast, and there was a great piece of Cold Boiled, and there were mince-pies, and plenty of beer. But the great effect of the evening came after the Roast and Boiled, when the fiddler (an artful dog, mind! The sort of man who knew his business better than you or I could have told it him!) struck up 'Sir Roger de Coverley'. Then old Fezziwig stood out to dance with Mrs Fezziwig. Top couple, too; with a good stiff piece of work cut out for them; three or four and twenty pair of partners; people who were not to be trifled with; people who would dance, and had no notion of walking.

But if they had been twice as many: ah, four times: old Fezziwig would have been a match for them, and so would Mrs Fezziwig. As to her, she was worthy to be his partner in every sense of the term. If that's not high praise, tell me higher, and I'll use it. A positive light appeared to issue from Fezziwig's calves. They shone in every part of the dance like moons. You couldn't have predicted, at any given time, what would become of 'em next. And when old Fezziwig and Mrs Fezziwig had gone all through the dance; advance and retire, hold hands with your partner; bow and curtsey; corkscrew; thread-the-needle, and back again to your place; Fezziwig 'cut' – cut so deftly, that he appeared to wink with his legs, and came upon his feet again without a stagger.

When the clock struck eleven, this domestic ball broke up. Mr and Mrs Fezziwig took their stations, one on either side the door, and shaking hands with every person individually as he or she went out, wished him or her a Merry Christmas. When everybody had retired but the two 'prentices, they did the same to them; and thus the cheerful voices died away, and the lads were left to their beds; which were under a counter in the back-shop.

A Christmas Crossword

Maggie Lane

This crossword comes from Maggie Lane's entertaining Charles Dickens Quiz and Puzzle Book, *published by Abson Books of Bristol in 1986.*
(For the answers, turn to page 121.)

Across

1 'There seems a — in the very name of Christmas' (5)
3 Scrooge '— his coffee in the dog days' (4)
6 'Every idiot who goes about with "Merry Christmas" on his lips, should be buried with a stake of — through his heart' (5)
7 Victorian innovation for putting presents round (4)
8 One of seven that, leafless, adorns the winter landscape (3)
9 Seasonal bird (5)
12 The Cratchits could not afford to — their own 25 (3)
13 Scrooge's remorse and pity — as the three Spirits of Christmas visited him (4)
14 On Christmas Eve at Dingley Dell it was the custom to '— the time with forfeits and old stories' (7)
17 Christmas trees are this (3)
19 Tiny diminutive boy (3)
20 'A rough but — and not unpleasant kind of music, scraping the snow from the pavement' (5)
24 'Christmas Eve at Cloisterham, — profusion in the shops' (6)
25 An alternative to goose (6)

Down

1 His ghost dragged a heavy chain (6)
2 Mr Grewgious's Christmas dinner consisted of boiled turkey with — sauce (6)
3 'Holly, mistletoe, red berries, —, turkeys, geese, game' (3)
4 Consuming occupation on Christmas Day (6)

5 'Sausages, oysters, —, puddings, fruit and punch, all vanished instantly' (4)

6 Scrooge's opinion of Christmas. Sweet? (6)

10 'It is good to — children sometimes, and never better than at Christmas' (2)

11 'Seasonable tokens are about. Red — shine here and there in the lattices' (7)

14 Fifteen of these were Bob Cratchit's weekly wage (3)

15 Used by Bob in Scrooge's ledgers (3)

16 Mr Wardle's daughter courted by Snodgrass at Christmas (5)

18 'I will honour Christmas in my heart, and try to keep — all the year' (2)

21 Another word for six down? Rubbish! (3)

22 Correct way for Bob to address Scrooge (3)

23 Day before or night when family and servants sit down together at Dingley Dell (3)

The Two Worthies

Charles Dickens

Christmas morning at Dingley Dell, and a memorable meeting in
The Pickwick Papers – the breakfast at which Mr Pickwick and Bob
Sawyer become acquainted for the first time.

'Well, Sam,' said Mr Pickwick as that favoured servitor entered his
bedchamber with his warm water, on the morning of Christmas Day,
'still frosty?'

'Water in the wash-hand basin's a mask o'ice, sir,' responded Sam.

'Severe weather, Sam,' observed Mr Pickwick.

'Fine time for them as is well wropped up, as the Polar Bear said to
himself, ven he was practising his skating,' replied Mr Weller.

'I shall be down in a quarter of an hour, Sam,' said Mr Pickwick, untying
his nightcap.

'Wery good, sir,' replied Sam. 'Ther's a couple o' Sawbones down-stairs.'

'A couple of what!' exclaimed Mr Pickwick, sitting up in bed.

'A couple o' Sawbones,' said Sam.

'What's a Sawbones?' inquired Mr Pickwick, not quite certain whether it
was a live animal, or something to eat.

'What! don't you know what a Sawbones is, sir?' inquired Mr Weller;
'I thought everybody know'd as a Sawbones was a Surgeon.'

'Oh, a Surgeon, eh?' said Mr Pickwick with a smile.

'Just that, sir,' replied Sam. 'These here ones as is below, though, ain't
reg'lar thoroughbred Sawbones; they're only in trainin'.'

'In other words, they're Medical Students, I suppose?' said Mr Pickwick.

Sam Weller nodded assent.

'I am glad of it,' said Mr Pickwick, casting his nightcap energetically on
the counterpane. 'They are fine fellows; very fine fellows; with judgments
matured by observation and reflection; and tastes refined by reading and
study. I am very glad of it.'

'They're a smokin' cigars by the kitchen fire,' said Sam.

'Ah!' observed Mr Pickwick, rubbing his hands, 'overflowing with kindly
feelings and animal spirits. Just what I like to see!'

'And one on 'em,' said Sam, not noticing his master's interruption, 'one on 'em's got his legs on the table, and is a drinkin' brandy neat, vile the t'other one – him in the barnacles – has got a barrel o' oysters atween his knees, wich he's a openin' like steam, and as fast as he eats 'em, he takes a aim vith the shells at young Dropsy, who's a sittin' down fast asleep in the chimbley corner.'

'Eccentricities of genius, Sam,' said Mr Pickwick. 'You may retire.'

Sam did retire accordingly; Mr Pickwick, at the expiration of a quarter of an hour, went down to breakfast.

'Here he is at last,' said old Wardle. 'Pickwick, this is Miss Allen's brother, Mr Benjamin Allen – Ben we call him, and so may you if you like. This gentleman is his very particular friend, Mr —.'

'Mr Bob Sawyer,' interposed Mr Benjamin Allen; whereupon Mr Bob Sawyer and Mr Benjamin Allen laughed in concert.

Mr Pickwick bowed to Bob Sawyer, and Bob Sawyer bowed to

Bob Sawyer's finest hour, on the roof of the chaise.

Mr Pickwick; Bob and his very particular friend then applied themselves most assiduously to the eatables before them; and Mr Pickwick had an opportunity of glancing at them both.

Mr Benjamin Allen was a coarse, stout, thick-set young man, with black hair cut rather short, and a white face cut rather long. He was embellished with spectacles, and wore a white neckerchief. Below his single-breasted black surtout, which was buttoned up to his chin, appeared the usual number of pepper-and-salt coloured legs, terminating in a pair of imperfectly polished boots. Although his coat was short in the sleeves, it disclosed no vestige of a linen wristband; and although there was quite enough of his face to admit of the encroachment of a shirt collar, it was not graced by the smallest approach to that appendage. He presented, altogether, rather a mildewy appearance; and emitted a fragrant odour of full-flavoured Cubas.

Mr Bob Sawyer, who was habited in a coarse blue coat, which, without being either a great-coat or a surtout, partook of the nature and qualities of both, had about him that sort of slovenly smartness, and swaggering gait, which is peculiar to young gentlemen who smoke in the streets by day, shout and scream in the same by night, call waiters by their Christian names, and do various other acts and deeds of an equally facetious description. He wore a pair of plaid trousers, and a large rough double-breasted waistcoat; and out of doors, carried a thick stick with a big top. He eschewed gloves: and looked, upon the whole, something like a dissipated Robinson Crusoe.

Such were the two worthies to whom Mr Pickwick was introduced, as he took his seat at the breakfast table on Christmas morning.

Stopped Payment

E l i z a b e t h   G a s k e l l

Mrs Gaskell, born in London but brought up in the Midlands and North, was very much one of Dickens' literary circle. Two of her finest novels, North and South *and* Cranford, *from which this excerpt is taken, were first published in his weekly* Household Words, *and he liked to call her* Mary Barton, *after the book that made her name in 1848. Later he*

*was heard to say that if he had been her husband he would have been
moved to beat her, but fortunately for her she was already spoken for.
William Gaskell was a celebrated minister at Manchester's Unitarian
Cross Street Chapel, one of a long line of brilliant clergy from that
denomination who contributed much to the city's cultural life.*

The very Tuesday morning on which Mr Johnson was going to show the
fashions, the post-woman brought two letters to the house. I say the post-
woman, but I should say the postman's wife. He was a lame shoemaker, a very
clean, honest man, much respected in the town; but he never brought the letters
round except on unusual occasions, such as Christmas Day, or Good Friday; and
on those days the letters, which should have been delivered at eight in the
morning, did not make their appearance until two or three in the afternoon; for
every one liked poor Thomas, and gave him a welcome on these festive
occasions. He used to say, 'He was well stawed wi' eating, for there were three or
four houses where nowt would serve 'em but he must share in their breakfast';
and by the time he had done his last breakfast, he came to some other friend who
was beginning dinner; but come what might in the way of temptation, Tom was
always sober, civil, and smiling; and, as Miss Jenkyns used to say, it was a lesson
in patience, that she doubted not would call out that precious quality in some
minds, where, but for Thomas, it might have lain dormant and undiscovered.

Patience was certainly very dormant in Miss Jenkyns's mind. She was always
expecting letters, and always drumming on the table till the post-woman had
called or gone past. On Christmas Day and Good Friday she drummed from
breakfast till church, from church-time till two o'clock – unless when the fire
wanted stirring, when she invariably knocked down the fire-irons, and scolded
Miss Matty for it. But equally certain was the hearty welcome and the good
dinner for Thomas; Miss Jenkyns standing over him like a bold dragoon,
questioning him as to his children – what they were doing – what school they
went to; upbraiding him if another was likely to make its appearance, but
sending even the little babies the shilling and the mince-pie which was her gift to
all the children, with half-a-crown in addition for both father and mother. The
post was not half of so much consequence to dear Miss Matty; but not for the
world would she have diminished Thomas's welcome and his dole, though
I could see that she felt rather shy over the ceremony, which had been regarded
by Miss Jenkyns as a glorious opportunity for giving advice and benefiting her
fellow-creatures. Miss Matty would steal the money all in a lump into his hand,

as if she were ashamed of herself. Miss Jenkyns gave him each individual coin separate, with a 'There! that's for yourself; that's for Jenny', &c. Miss Matty would even beckon Martha out of the kitchen while he ate his food: and once, to my knowledge, winked at its rapid disappearance into a blue cotton pocket-handkerchief. Miss Jenkyns almost scolded him if he did not leave a clean plate, however heaped it might have been, and gave an injunction with every mouthful.

A Fern for Every Guest

The Woman at Home magazine was good not only for elaborate recipes but for some bright ideas on festive table decorations. Presuming that those who produced it knew their market, what a luxury of leisure hours comfortably-off women enjoyed in Victorian times!

Now that the flower gardens are nearly desolate, we must go to the shrubbery, the woods, or the conservatory for leaves to embellish our table and as our dinner is a Christmas one, the place of honour must be given to the holly, which with an abundance of its red berries might be put in a round or oval dish in the centre of the table. To take off the rather hard metallic look of the leaves put mistletoe along with it. Half way down the table place a plant of white camellia or azalea with maidenhair fern on both sides and, if it can be procured, a poinsettia might be placed near the top of the table, that is, if the table is a large one. At each guest's place put a small, narrow glass vase with a piece of maidenhair fern and mistletoe, or the fern and a small sprig of straw-coloured holly.

Fold the table-napkins in the mitre shape, and put a tiny piece of holly with berries on each. If the poinsettia be on the table, the embroidered table centre, if one be used, should have plenty of blue in it; should the plants be white or pale pink azaleas, the embroidery might be of Indian red and gold.

Joy and Ecstasy

Charles Dickens

Scrooge might have married Belle, but did not. Here the Ghost of Christmas Past shows him the family life that he missed in a passage that encapsulates the Victorians' sentimental view of domestic bliss, especially during the festive season.

But now a knocking at the door was heard, and such a rush immediately ensued that she with laughing face and plundered dress was borne towards it the centre of a flushed and boisterous group, just in time to greet the father, who came home attended by a man laden with Christmas toys and presents. Then the shouting and the struggling, and the onslaught that was made on the defenceless porter! The scaling him with chairs for ladders to dive into his pockets, despoil him of brown-paper parcels, hold on tight by his cravat, hug him round the neck, pommel his back, and kick his legs in irrepressible affection!

The shouts of wonder and delight with which the development of every package was received! The terrible announcement that the baby had been taken in the act of putting a doll's frying-pan into his mouth, and was more than suspected of having swallowed a fictitious turkey, glued on a wooden platter! The immense relief of finding this a false alarm! The joy, and gratitude, and ecstasy! They are all indescribable alike. It is enough that by degrees the children and their emotions got out of the parlour and by one stair at a time, up to the top of the house; where they went to bed, and so subsided.

Chaffed on Skates

Francis Kilvert

Dickens was dead by the end of 1870, but as this excerpt from Kilvert's Diary *shows, country house Christmases lived on. The Revd Francis Kilvert is one of the most celebrated of Victorian diarists, remembered not least for an affection for young girls in a manner reminiscent of Lewis Carroll. This Christmas sees him at home for the holiday with his parents in Wiltshire, surely a rare treat at this busiest of times for clergymen.*

Sunday, Christmas Day 1870

As I lay awake praying in the early morning I thought I heard a sound of distant bells. It was an intense frost. I sat down in my bath upon a sheet of thick ice which broke in the middle into large pieces whilst sharp points and jagged edges stuck all around the sides of the tub like chevaux de frise, not particularly comfortable to the naked thighs and loins, for the keen ice cut like broke glass. The ice water stung and scorched like fire. I had to collect the frozen pieces of ice and pile them on a chair before I could use the sponge and then I had to thaw the sponge in my hands for it was a mass of ice. The morning was brilliant. Walked to the Sunday School with Gibbins and the road sparkled with millions of rainbows, the seven colours gleaming in every glittering point of hoar frost. The church was very cold in spite of two roaring stove fires.

Mr Pickwick on ice 'amidst the gratified shouts of all the spectators'.

Tuesday, 27 December

After dinner drove into Chippenham with Perch and bought two pair of skates at Benk's for 17s 6d. Across the fields to the Draycot water and the young Awdry ladies chaffed me about my new skates. I had not been on skates since I was here last, five years ago, and was very awkward for the first ten minutes, but the knack soon came again. There was a distinguished company on the ice, Lady Dangan, Lord and Lady Royston and Lord George Paget all skating. Also Lord and Lady Sydney and a Mr Calcroft, whom they all of course called the Hangman. I had the honour of being knocked down by Lord Royston, who was coming round suddenly on the outside edge. A large fire of logs burning within an enclosure of wattled hurdles. Harriet Awdry skated beautifully and jumped over a half-sunken punt. Arthur Law skating jumped over a chair on its legs.

Wednesday, 28 December

An inch of snow fell last night and as we walked to Draycot to skate the storm began again. As we passed Langley Burrell Church we heard the strains of the quadrille band on the ice at Draycot. The afternoon grew murky and when we began to skate the air was thick with falling snow. But it soon stopped and gangs of labourers were at work immediately sweeping away the new fallen snow. The Lancers was beautifully skated. When it grew dark the ice was lighted with Chinese lanterns, and the intense glare of blue, green and crimson lights and magnesium riband made the whole place as light as day. Then people skated with torches.

Nothing Could be Heartier

Charles Dickens

Scrooge is saved, the spirit of Christmas is upon him – and the mere rhythm and pace of Dickens' narrative tell us all we need to know about the joy in his heart and the spring in his step in this exhilarating passage from A Christmas Carol.

He went to church, and walked about the streets, and watched the people hurrying to and fro, and patted children on the head and questioned beggars, and looked down into the kitchens of houses, and up to the windows, and found that everything could yield him pleasure. He had never dreamed that any walk – that anything – could give him so much happiness. In the afternoon he turned his steps towards his nephew's house.

'Is your master at home, my dear?' said Scrooge to the girl.

'He's in the dining-room, sir, along with the mistress. I'll show you upstairs, if you please.'

'Thank 'ee. He knows me,' said Scrooge, with his hand already on the dining-room lock. 'I'll go in here, my dear.'

'Why bless my soul!' cried Fred, 'who's that?'

'It's I. Your uncle Scrooge. I have come to dinner. Will you let me in, Fred?'

Let him in! It's a mercy he didn't shake his arm off. He was at home in five minutes. Nothing could be heartier. His niece looked just the same. So did Topper when he came. So did the plump sister when she came. So did every one when they came. Wonderful party, wonderful games, wonderful unanimity, wonderful happiness!

But he was early at the office next morning. Oh, he was early there. If only he could be there first, and catch Bob Cratchit coming late! That was the thing he had set his heart on.

And he did it; yes, he did! The clock struck nine. No Bob. A quarter past. No Bob. He was full eighteen minutes and a half behind his time. Scrooge sat with his door wide open, that he might see him coming into the office. His hat was off, before he opened the door; his comforter too. He was on his stool in a jiffy; driving away with his pen, as if he were trying to overtake nine o'clock.

'Hallo!' growled Scrooge, in his accustomed voice, as near as he could feign it. 'What do you mean by coming here at this time of day?'

'I am very sorry, sir,' said Bob. 'I am behind my time.'

'You are?' repeated Scrooge. 'Yes. I think you are. Step this way, sir, if you please.'

'It's only once a year, sir,' pleaded Bob, appearing from the office. 'It shall not be repeated. I was making rather merry yesterday, sir.'

'Now, I'll tell you what, my friend,' said Scrooge, 'I am not going to stand this sort of thing any longer. And therefore,' he continued, leaping from his stool, and giving Bob such a dig in the waistcoat that he staggered back into the office again; 'and therefore I am about to raise your salary! A merry Christmas, Bob!' said Scrooge, with an earnestness that could not be mistaken, as he clapped him on the back. 'A merrier Christmas, Bob, my good fellow, than I have given you for many a year! I'll raise your salary, and endeavour to assist your struggling family, and we will discuss your affairs this very afternoon, over a Christmas bowl of smoking bishop, Bob! Make up the fires, and buy another coal-scuttle before you dot another i, Bob Cratchit!'

Swidgers by the Score

Charles Dickens

Yet another Dickensian Christmas dinner – but an eerie one, from
The Haunted Man.

Then, as Christmas is a time in which, of all times in the year, the memory of every remediable sorrow, wrong, and trouble in the world around us, should be active with us, not less than our own experiences, for all good, he laid his hand upon the boy, and, silently calling Him to witness who laid His hand on children in old time, rebuking, in the majesty of His prophetic knowledge, those who kept them from Him, vowed to protect him, teach him, and reclaim him.

Then, as he gave his right hand cheerily to Philip, and said that they would that day hold a Christmas dinner in what used to be, before the ten poor gentlemen commuted, their great Dinner Hall; and that they would bid to it as many of that Swidger family, who, his son had told him, were so numerous that they might join hands and make a ring round England, as could be brought together on so short a notice.

And it was that day done. There were so many Swidgers there, grown up and with children, that an attempt to state them in round numbers might engender doubts, in the distrustful, of the veracity of this history. Therefore the attempt shall not be made. But there they were, by dozens and scores – and there was good news and good hope there, ready for them, of George, who had been visited again by his father and brother, and by Milly, and again left in a quiet sleep. There, present at the dinner, too, were the Tetterbys, including young Adolphus, who arrived in his prismatic comforter, in good time for the beef. Johnny and the baby were too late, of course, and came in all on one side, the one exhausted, the other in a supposed state of double-tooth; but that was customary, and not alarming.

It was sad to see the child who had no name or lineage, watching the other children as they played, not knowing how to talk with them, or sport with them, and more strange to the ways of childhood than a rough dog. It was sad, though in a different way, to see what an instinctive knowledge the

youngest children there, had of his being different from all the rest, and how they made timid approaches to him with soft words and touches, and with little presents, that he might not be unhappy. But he kept by Milly, and began to love her – that was another, as she said! – and, as they all liked her dearly, they were glad of that, and when they saw him peeping at them from behind her chair, they were pleased that he was so close to it.

All this, the Chemist, sitting with the student and his bride that was to be, and Philip, and the rest, saw.

Some people have said since, that he only thought what has been herein set down; others, that he read it in the fire, one winter night about the twilight time; others, that the Ghost was but the representation of his better wisdom. I say nothing.

Except this. That as they were assembled in the old Hall, by no other light than that of the great fire (having dined early), the shadows once more stole out of their hiding-places, and danced about the room, showing the children marvellous shapes and faces on the walls, and gradually changing what was real and familiar there, to what was wild and magical. But that there was one thing in the Hall, to which the eyes of Redlaw, and of Milly and her husband, and of the old man, and of the student, and his bride that was to be, were often turned, which the shadows did not obscure or change. Deepened in its gravity by the firelight, gazing from the darkness of the panelled wall like life, the sedate face in the portrait, with the beard and ruff, looked down at them from under its verdant wreath of holly, as they looked up at it; and, clear and plain below, as if a voice had uttered them, were the words, 'Lord keep my memory green'.

What Christmas Is, As We Grow Older

Charles Dickens

Writing in the 1851 Christmas issue of Household Words, *Dickens introduced a series of 'What Christmas Is' essays with a thoughtful piece, part of which is reproduced here. It should be remembered that he was not yet forty when he wrote it – a reflection of both the Victorian concept of ageing and the way in which his body was finding it hard to keep pace with his frantic lifestyle.*

Time was, with most of us, when Christmas Day encircling all our limited world like a magic ring, left nothing out for us to miss or seek; bound together all our home enjoyments, affections, and hopes; grouped every thing and every one around the Christmas fire; and made the little picture shining in our bright young eyes, complete.

Time came, perhaps, all so soon! when our thoughts overleaped that narrow boundary; when there was some one (very dear, we thought then, very beautiful, and absolutely perfect) wanting to the fulness of our happiness; when we were wanting too (or we thought so, which did just as well) at the Christmas hearth by which that some one sat; and when we intertwined with every wreath and garland of our life that some one's name.

The Private View, Illustrated London News, *23 December 1865.*

That was the time for the bright, visionary Christmases which have long arisen from us to shew faintly, after summer rain, in the palest edges of the rainbow! That was the time for the beatified enjoyment of the things that were to be, and never were, and yet the things that were so real in our resolute hope that it would be hard to say, now, what realities achieved since, have been stronger!

What! Did that Christmas never really come when we and the priceless pearl who was our young choice were received, after the happiest of totally impossible marriages, by the two united families previously at daggers-drawn on our account? When brothers and sisters in law who had always been rather cool to us before our relationship was effected, perfectly doted on us, and when fathers and mothers overwhelmed us with unlimited incomes? Was that Christmas dinner never really eaten, after which we arose, and generously and eloquently rendered honour to our late rival, present in the company, then and there exchanging friendship and forgiveness, and founding an attachment, not to be surpassed in Greek or Roman story, which subsisted until death? Has that same rival long ceased to care for that same priceless pearl, and married for money, and become usurious? Above all, do we really know, now, that we should probably have been miserable if we had won and worn the pearl, and that we are better without her?

That Christmas when we had recently achieved so much fame; when we had been carried in triumph somewhere, for doing something great and good; when we had won an honoured and ennobled name, and arrived and were received at home in a shower of tears of joy; is it possible that that Christmas has not come yet?

And is our life here, at the best, so constituted that, pausing as we advance at such a noticeable mile-stone in the track as this great birthday, we look back on the things that never were, as naturally and full as gravely as on the things that have been and are gone, or have been and still are? If it be so, and so it seems to be, must we come to the conclusion, that life is little better than a dream, and little worth the loves and strivings that we crowd into it?

No! Far be such miscalled philosophy from us, dear Reader, on Christmas Day! Nearer and closer to our hearts be the Christmas spirit, which is the spirit of active usefulness, perseverance, cheerful discharge of duty, kindness, and forbearance! It is in the last virtues especially, that we are, or should be strengthened by the unaccomplished visions of our youth; for, who shall say that they are not our teachers to deal gently even with the impalpable nothings of the earth!

Therefore, as we grow older, let us be more thankful that the circle of our Christmas associations and of the lessons that they bring, expands! Let us welcome every one of them, and summon them to take their places by the Christmas hearth.

Welcome, old aspirations, glittering creatures of an ardent fancy, to your shelter underneath the holly! We know you, and have not outlived you yet. Welcome, old projects and old loves, however fleeting, to your nooks among the steadier lights that burn around us. Welcome, all that was ever real to our hearts; and for the earnestness that made you real, thanks to Heaven! Do we build no Christmas castles in the clouds now? Let our thoughts, fluttering like butterflies among these flowers of children, bear witness! Before this boy, there stretches out a Future, brighter than we ever looked on in our old romantic time, but bright with honour and with truth. Around this little head on which the sunny curls lie heaped, the graces sport, as prettily, as airily, as when there was no scythe within the reach of Time to shear away the curls of our first-love. Upon another girl's face near it – placider but smiling bright – a quiet and contented little face, we see Home fairly written. Shining from the word, as rays shine from a star, we see how, when our graves are old, other hopes than ours are young, other hearts than ours are moved; how other ways are smoothed; how other happiness blooms, ripens, and decays – no, not decays, for other homes and other bands of children, not yet in being nor for ages yet to be, arise, and bloom and ripen to the end of all!

The Song of the Shirt

Thomas Hood

Thomas Hood, who died young in 1845, is best remembered as a poet today, though in his lifetime he earned his living as a journalist in London, specializing in light, comical fare. Clearly his world was very much that of Dickens, and the two knew and liked one another, to the extent that Hood was one of the chosen few friends Dickens delighted in mimicking. This poem was published in the Christmas edition of Punch *magazine in 1843, the year of* A Christmas Carol, *and says much about the growing awareness of social issues among the middle classes of that decade, especially at Christmas time. It was a year later that Dickens published* The Chimes, *an equally stinging onslaught on the exploitation of the weak and helpless.*

With fingers weary and worn,
With eyelids heavy and red,
A Woman sat, in unwomanly rags,
Plying her needle and thread –
Stitch! stitch! stitch!
In poverty, hunger, and dirt,
And still with a voice of dolorous pitch
She sang the 'Song of the Shirt!'

'Work! work! work!
While the cock is crowing aloof!
And work – work – work,
Till the stars shine through the roof!
It's O! to be a slave
Along with the barbarous Turk,
Where woman has never a soul to save,
If this is Christian work!

'Work – work – work
Till the brain begins to swim;
Work – work – work
Till the eyes are heavy and dim!
Seam, and gusset, and band,
Band, and gusset, and seam,
Till over the buttons I fall asleep,
And sew them on in a dream!

'O! Men, with Sisters dear!
O! Men! with Mothers and Wives!
It is not linen you're wearing out,
But human creatures' lives!
Stitch – stitch – stitch,
In poverty, hunger, and dirt,
Sewing at once, with a double thread,
A Shroud as well as a Shirt.

'But why do I talk of Death?
That Phantom of grisly bone,
I hardly fear his terrible shape,
It seems so like my own –
It seems so like my own,
Because of the fasts I keep,
Oh! God! that bread should be so dear,
And flesh and blood so cheap!

'Work – work – work!
My labour never flags;
And what are its wages? A bed of straw,
A crust of bread – and rags.
That shatter'd roof – and this naked floor –
A table – a broken chair –
And a wall so blank, my shadow I thank
For sometimes falling there!

'Work – work – work!
From weary chime to chime,
Work – work – work,
As prisoners work for crime!
Band, and gusset, and seam,
Seam, and gusset, and band,
Till the heart is sick, and the brain benumb'd,
As well as the weary hand.

'Work – work – work,
In the dull December light,
And work – work – work,
When the weather is warm and bright –
While underneath the eaves
The brooding swallows cling
As if to show me their sunny backs
And twit me with the spring.

'Oh! but to breathe the breath
Of the cowslip and primrose sweet –
With the sky above my head,
And the grass beneath my feet,
For only one short hour
To feel as I used to feel,
Before I knew the woes of want
And the walk that costs a meal!

'Oh but for one short hour!
A respite however brief!
No blessed leisure for Love or Hope,
But only time for Grief!
A little weeping would ease my heart,
But in their briny bed
My tears must stop, for every drop
Hinders needle and thread!'

With fingers weary and worn,
With eyelids heavy and red,
A Woman sat in unwomanly rags,
Plying her needle and thread –
Stitch! stitch! stitch!
In poverty, hunger, and dirt,
And still with a voice of dolorous pitch,
Would that its tone could reach the Rich!
She sang this 'Song of the Shirt!'

Some Compliments of the Season

This piece, published anonymously in a Christmas issue of Household Words *in the middle of the last century, combines two familiar Dickensian themes, the lively Christmas shops and the plight of the poor during the season of goodwill.*

As we trudge through the streets everybody seems to be eating and drinking, or preparing to eat and drink. The crossing sweeper munches a huge parallelepipedon of bread and treacle, bestowed on him, no doubt, by some kindly spinster in the neighbourhood; the policeman leans somewhat lazily against a railing, notwithstanding the cold. He looks plethoric, dyspeptic. Goodness! what number of supports has that municipal officer consumed with what number of cooks? How many puddings, in their raw state, has he tasted? How many sly little nuggets off noble joints have been broiled for him? How many sausages – links in that chain which binds the turkey to our heart – will be missing to-morrow, owing to his Christmas Eve rapacity? Will X 99 dine? Of course he will; and Mrs Policeman X 99 is at this moment concluding the purchase of a mighty piece of pork and a colossal amalgamation of cabbages, known in the precincts of Brill, Somers Town, where the transaction takes place, as a 'green': which pork and green will cheer the heart of honest X 99 when he comes off duty.

Strangers – a pauper girl and Father Christmas. Punch, *29 December 1883.*

As it grows later on Christmas Eve, hot elder wine comes out at corners of streets. A polished, brazen urn sends up a fragrant steam in the midst of lamps, and glasses, and heaps of rusks; while its proprietor, boasting of its power to make the coldest individual as warm as a toast in one moment, swings his arms across his chest, and runs to and fro, in front of his establishment, with a blueness of nose that rather exposes the weakness of his case to thoughtful minds. I have time to turn down one of the alleys in this neighbourhood. I have known this part from childhood. It is not much changed since I thought it a lawless place, inhabited chiefly by boys with whom my white collar and general cleanliness were the unfortunate causes of much irritation. Some weavers live in it; as frequent announcements of 'Rooms to let, with standing for loom and quilling, at three shillings per week', will confirm. But the majority are cabinet-makers – sallow men, whose hair and clothes are full of mahogany dust.

Some of them buy bits of wood cheap, and make up complete articles to be sold as soon as made, for anything they will fetch. Others make only some portion of an article, of which they scarcely know the use, and by long habit grow swift-fingered, to keep up with falling prices. Out of their branch of labour, they are for the most part stupid. Mangling seems to be done everywhere. Children are taken in to mind at twopence per day. There is a court with the announcement, 'Small houses to let up this passage, at three shillings and sixpence per week.' But the houses in this poor neighbourhood are mostly high. Some have once been a kind of mansion, when perhaps there were few houses near. They stood at that time, very likely, in gardens, and in the midst of fields; for of the once rural character of the neighbourhood the names of streets and places still tell. One of these is now inhabited by some twenty poor families, and has strangely fallen from its old gentility. Another is shut up; perhaps too ruinous for habitation. Every window in the front is broken, in consequence of a ghost which has been seen there at various times – off and on – for some years past. There seems a general love of animals in these parts. Dog-fanciers are in every street, and stuffers of birds, beasts, and fishes. One of them exhibits a cat with two heads in a glass-case, as well as a canine coincidence with the Siamese twins. The canine twins I suspect to have been strangers to each other previously to their decease.

Christmas at the Workhouse

'One Who Has Seen Better Days'

Local scandal sheets had a tremendous vogue in later Victorian times, and if 'The Owl' in Nottingham did nothing else of lasting worth, it left us this astonishing documentary evidence of life in that city's York Street workhouse in the 1880s. Published in the Christmas Day number of 1886, it is remarkable for painting the picture from the point of view of an inmate, rather than of the board officials or of well-meaning visitors who, as the writer reflects, saw an extremely rosy version of events on their Christmas Day visits. Of course the account is partial – the magazine was proudly anti-establishment – but it nevertheless rings true. Interestingly, it is almost exactly contemporary with George R. Sims' 'Christmas Day in the Workhouse', a ballad which, for all its openness to parody, was a savage indictment of the Poor Law of 1834. Obviously, liberal thinking of the 1880s was swinging violently against the system, as had Dickens' several decades before that – yet it was not until 1929, in the lifetime of our Queen, that it was erased from the statute book.

It is necessary that the reader should be carried on 'fancy's wings' through the portals and into the precincts of the workhouse before he can fully realize the picture of its interior life. I write from actual experience, and may be able to take the perusers of this article, in thought, with me. As one of the unfortunate individuals whom the great depression of trade has driven for shelter within the grim enclosure situated in York Street, Nottingham, I will attempt to give the reader a truthful and graphic description. Let me confine myself to an outline of facts. Reduced to the greatest straits, and desirous of keeping in the path of rectitude, I was compelled to seek relief at the hands of our indulgent ratepayers, and accordingly turned my steps towards York Street. Entering the waiting room adjoining the relieving officers' sanctums, I found myself surrounded by a group of women wanting to receive in turn their weekly outdoor dole. I stood some time expecting a call from one of the occupants of the sacred office, but to my surprise found myself forestalled by an able-bodied man who had come on the same quest.

Presently my ears were offended by uncouth language issuing apparently from one of the said sanctums. 'Well, what do you want?' queried an individual from behind the partition, with all the pomposity of a parish beadle.

'I want an order for admission to the house, as I am quite destitute.'

'Destitute? A strong, able man like you, destitute? Why, I should be ashamed of myself to come and sponge on the ratepayers if I were like you' – forgetting that he is one of the greatest sponges on the ratepayers.

After further bullying and browbeating the unfortunate applicant was asked 'Where did you sleep last night?' The reply not being satisfactory to the bumptious officer, that personage said: 'Well, you'll have to go into the Tramp Ward before you can get an order here.'

On hearing this I slipped out of the office, strolled pensively round the Forest, then unconsciously headed Carrington way, wondering all the time why it seemed imperative that a man should have a course of 'crummy' in the Tramp Ward before he was considered a fit candidate for admission into the body of the house. There was no alternative for me but to seek the Tramp Ward at night. Next morning but one, I presented myself before the officer of my district. He was apparently in a jovial humour, as he was humming the favourite air 'You'll Remember Me', while the officer in the adjoining department glanced towards me with a scowl as black as night through his official goggles. My appearance at the pigeon hole somewhat altered the tone of the singing man. Even a good fellow like him has to assume the regulation frown on such occasions, while the massive carbuncle ring he wore reminded me painfully that I too had once been coxcomb enough to bedizen my fingers. He condescended to ask my business, I explained my case and the usual verbosity followed. Not wishing to bandy words, I had qualified myself by gathering a 'few friends' to take in with me, so the admission order was granted, and I was permitted to enter the house. I was received the same night into the able-bodied 'day ward', a full-blown, fustian-clad pauper.

I was presented with a tin medal to be hung over my bed, on which was pasted a number corresponding to the one on my shirt, stockings, and neckerchief. How do you like my suit? A pair of trousers with no pockets, a vest ditto, a jacket with a solitary button and button-hole, and – no it ain't – yes it is – a miniature pocket, justly supposed to be a sufficiently commodious receptacle to contain all the heterogeneous mass of an indoor pauper's property. A piece of rag for a pocket handkerchief, as he is not supplied with that necessary article, a comb, a piece of soap, pipe and tobacco, needles, thread, any scraps of food, are crammed indiscriminately into this apology for a pocket which adorns the pauper's jacket. No wonder that the ingenious contrive clandestine pouches in

the linings of the vests, as even in a workhouse there are men who have feelings of common decency left, and do not care to have their food mixed with small tooth comb, carbolic soap and mucous wiper. The able-bodied ward, styled 'No. 2 Day Ward', is a room about eighteen or twenty feet by about ten feet. In this space are crammed about eighty men. The stifling atmosphere is something to remember. On my entrance I found that active preparations were being made for the annual festival. Coloured paper in profusion had been kindly given by Messrs Goater, Ford, and other local firms, whilst plenty of holly and other evergreens had been contributed by his Grace the Duke of St Albans, Colonel Seely, Mr Clifton, Captain Holden and other country gentlemen.

An old soldier – whose taste in decorative and other artistic work is deserving of a better sphere – was preparing the various devices for ornamenting the large dinner hall and other principal parts of the house. One of the assistant bakers was also busy in a similar manner, brightening the old men's ward. Several precepts and texts were arranged on the ward walls, one in particular being noticeable, the threadbare quotation: 'He that giveth to the poor, lendeth to the Lord.' For some reason, the worthy Boss of the House ordered another one to be substituted, which met with his approval. It was singularly suggestive, being worded: 'Come let us join our

A Christmas Party: Poor. Illustrated London News, *25 December 1886.*

friends above.' I could scarcely repress a smile on reading these words, as it occurred to my mind that this was a sly joke of the worthy governor's on the desirability – from the official point of view – of the rapid emigration of paupers to Spirit Land.

Christmas, it appears, had been the sole theme of conversation for months previous to my arrival, and various were the surmises as to how it would pass off. 'I wish it was Christmas tomorrow, for I ain't hed nowt to eat wuth a menshun sin I've bin in.' 'And I ain't either, and am longing for a bit o' bacca.' 'Roll on a pound o' plum duff, six ounce o' roast beef, a nounce o' bacca, and a pint of ale, and I shell last for a nuther twelve munth.' These and similar expressions are continually heard months before the great Feed arrives. Who can wonder, when one considers the paltry and insignificant amount of food which is doled out to the inmates? Even those Nottingham slaves who may be seen daily dragging a load of firewood, the weight of which, together with the cart, is equal to nearly half a ton, receive not an atom of extra food beyond the regular six ounces of bread and tin of skilly, morning and night. On Monday an extraordinary repast is provided for dinner, consisting of three ounces of bread and a tin of veritable dish-washings. In fact a candle stirred in a pot of boiling water would be far preferable to the swill served out as nourishing broth. On Tuesday and Thursday the dinner diet is four ounces of meat with potatoes boiled in their jackets. Fish was served every Thursday until the authorities saw that the inmates would rather 'clam' than eat it. This was no fault of the fish, as it was generally sound enough, but the manner of cooking and serving rendered it uneatable, even by the half-starved paupers.

Just fancy a whole head, with the gaping jaws and the glaring eye sockets, put upon one plate, the tail deposited on another, and a sickly admixture of flour and water poured over each mess. Instead of being eaten, the fish was often arranged into various devices on the plates. The tail of a finny 'un might be inserted into its jaws, and the whole deposited on a pedestal of the bones, presenting a curious spectacle to those officials who went through the dining hall after a fish dinner. On Monday the gigantic feast of three ounces of bread with a tin of pea soup is provided for the mid-day meal. On Fridays, the inmates luxuriate on a pound of pudding, with a sauce not unlike neatsfoot oil, seasoned with a little vinegar and sugar. On Saturdays a small quantity of Irish stew forms the extravagant repast.

Do not, therefore, wonder that the inmates look forward to the Christmas 'gorge' with the pleasure of hope, knowing that for once in the year the gnawing worm in their stomachs is likely to be stilled. The happy day at length arrives, and the breakfast for this eventful morning is more attractive to the skilly 'gorgers', as they receive tea instead of gruel, and are even presented with a quarter of an ounce of butter to their six-ounce 'cracker', morning and nights. After breakfast, divine service is held in the dinner hall, which in its ordinary state is a cold, cheerless, dark looking room that strikes a chill to the very bones as you enter it from the warm wards. It is certain that many a poor old man has had his days curtailed by having to get his food in such a damp and draughty place. On this occasion, however, what a contrast is presented! Festoons of evergreens hang around, stars and other devices occupy the vacant spaces, the long, bare gas pendants are dressed in an attractive manner – in fact the whole room is handsomely decorated. The chill even seems to be taken away, and a general warmth prevails.

Towards noon, visitors begin to arrive, for the express purpose of seeing the 'animals feed', and various are the comments heard, as to the extraordinary comforts provided for the pauper. These people only see the workhouse in its holiday attire, and are apt to be led astray by the apparent comfort, and even luxury, which the pauper enjoys. Superficial observers are likely to din into the ears of any poor creature who may apply to them for relief the well-known phrase: 'Go to the workhouse, you will be well cared for there.' In this case there are two sides to the picture, and I beg ratepayers who have looked only on the holiday side to take an opportunity of also examining the everyday reverse. Christmas Day is misleading, and so also are such days as those of Councillor Gregory's treat.

At last the dinner bell sounds and a general stampede commences towards the hall. Never, except on this and similar occasions, is there such a unanimous desire to enter the room. On the extreme right, as you enter the hall, are seated the young women, and to the left of them the old ladies in their snowy caps. The centre is occupied by the old gentlemen, attired on this occasion in their Sunday best. On the extreme left are ranged the young and able-bodied men, who with appetites keenly whetted, anxiously await the moment of attack, sniffing with evident delight the fumes of approaching roast beef.

Immediately grace is said, up fly four sliding doors, and the steaming edibles are carried by active paupers of both sexes to their respective contingents. Of course, the old ladies and gentlemen are first served, then the hungry young ones come in for their share. The six ounces of – for once – good roast beef, garnished with potatoes ready peeled, are supplied to each inmate. This allowance is soon demolished by the voracious able bodied, and the clatter of their knives and forks is stilled long before the old men have got through their job. Anxious glances are turned towards the sliding doors for the plum duff and coveted pint of ale (which latter would be debarred altogether if 'Windbag and Water-Melon' could have his way). Eventually, the efforts of the attacking force are relaxed, their faces look flushed, and they appear different individuals altogether.

Pieces of paper, pocket handkerchiefs and other wrappers are now produced for the purpose of gathering up the fragments of the repast, which are duly deposited in the solitary pocket I have described for future use. The pint of ale is drained, tobacco is served to the men, tea and sugar to the women, buns, oranges, sweets and so on to the children, and in about an hour from the commencement of the charge the battle is over. A member of the board arises and makes a 'few remarks' about as edifying as Maccabe's celebrated after-dinner speech. Then, after wishing all a Merry Christmas and a Happy New Year, a general exodus is made from the hall to the various wards, the young men shouting out: 'Roll on, next Christmas, for another feed.' In the evening divine service is again held, at which the harmony of Mr Copleston's choir is very welcome. Service over, the inmates again retire to their various wards and fight the day's battle o'er again. A little extra indulgence is granted on this occasion, and instead of all being in bed 'like good children' by eight o'clock, it is drawing towards ten before an ascent is made to the men's attic.

This retreat is a special feature of the house. It is a long room formed by the sloping of the roof. Innumerable baulks and supports intercept you at every few feet, and about eighty beds are generally occupied, about Christmas time, in that roosting place. The bedsteads are placed in every conceivable position, head to foot, side to head and so on, throughout its length and breadth, forming such a labyrinth that the poor old men who occupy a room at each end of the attic often get lost and scrape their poor old shins when they have to grope their way in the darkness. Economy forbids the use of a light except in the hospital or on the staircases.

Well, the reader can form some idea what a Babel of tongues is heard in the attic on this occasion, when the pint of ale has greased them. Comic songs and tales are sung and related, and occasional barking, mewing, crowing, and every conceivable kind of noise add to the general hubbub. All the hawkers' cries – 'Tops, swede tops', 'Watercress', 'Peas and Sausage', 'Salt' – and all the well known street cries are bellowed out with such lustiness as would make you fancy that the residents of Woodborough Road or York Street would not be able to sleep. 'Roll on, Walter Gregory's treat,' one will shout. 'I think it's cowd on that this year,' another will respond. 'Well, then, roll on, Jubilee, we shall get a feed then.' These and other larks are kept up till the midnight hour has chimed, and at length Morpheus claims his subjects one by one, until his hand closes the lips and eyes of the last of the yarning Mohicans.

Foul Weather for Trotty

Charles Dickens

This excerpt from the Christmas book The Chimes *gives a very different account of winter for the poor than the sentimental Christmas card image. As always with Dickens at his best, it is a little snapshot of street life in Victorian times in which, for once, a dozen words are worth a hundred pictures.*

Wet weather was the worst: the cold, damp, clammy wet, that wrapped him up like a moist great-coat: the only kind of great-coat Toby owned, or could have added to his comfort by dispensing with. Wet days, when the rain came slowly, thickly, obstinately down; when the street's throat, like his own, was choked with mist; when smoking umbrellas passed and repassed, spinning round and round like so many teetotums, as they knocked against each other on the crowded footway, throwing off a little whirlpool of uncomfortable sprinklings; when gutters brawled and waterspouts were full and noisy; when the wet from the projecting stones and ledges of the church fell drip, drip, drip, on Toby, making the wisp of straw on which he stood

mere mud in no time; those were the days that tried him. Then indeed, you might see Toby looking anxiously out from his shelter in an angle of the church wall – such a meagre shelter that in summer time it never cast a shadow thicker than a good-sized walking stick upon the sunny pavement – with a disconsolate and lengthened face. But coming out, a minute afterwards, to warm himself by exercise: and trotting up and down some dozen times: he would brighten even then, and go back more brightly to his niche.

They called him Trotty from his pace, which meant speed if it didn't make it. He could have walked faster perhaps; most likely; but rob him of his trot, and Toby would have taken to his bed and died. It bespattered him with mud in dirty weather; it cost him a world of trouble; he could have walked with infinitely greater ease; but that was one reason for his clinging to it so tenaciously. A weak, small, spare old man, he was a very Hercules, this Toby, in his good intentions. He loved to earn his money. He delighted to believe – Toby was very poor, and couldn't well afford to part with a delight – that he was worth his salt. With a shilling or an eighteen-penny message or small parcel in hand, his courage, always high, rose higher. As he trotted on, he would call out to fast Postmen ahead of him, to get out of the way; devoutly believing that in the natural course of things he must inevitably overtake and run them down; and he had perfect faith – not often tested – in his being able to carry anything that man could lift.

Thus, even when he came out of his nook to warm himself on a wet day, Toby trotted. Making, with his leaky shoes, a crooked line of slushy footprints in the mire; and blowing on his chilly hands and rubbing them against each other, poorly defended from the searching cold by threadbare mufflers of grey worsted, with a private apartment only for the thumb, and a common room or tap for the rest of the fingers; Toby, with his knees bent

and his cane beneath his arm, still trotted. Falling out into the road to look up at the belfry when the Chimes resounded, Toby trotted still.

He made this last excursion several times a day, for they were company to him; and when he heard their voices, he had an interest in glancing at their lodging-place, and thinking how they were moved, and what hammers beat upon them. Perhaps he was the more curious about these Bells, because there were points of resemblance between themselves and him. They hung there, in all weathers: with the wind and rain driving in upon them: facing only the outsides of all those houses; never getting any nearer to the blazing fires that gleamed and shone upon the windows, or came puffing out of the chimney tops; and incapable of participation in any of the good things that were constantly being handed, through the street doors and the area railings, to prodigious cooks. Faces came and went at many windows: sometimes pretty faces, youthful faces, pleasant faces: sometimes the reverse: but Toby knew no more (though he often speculated on these trifles, standing idle in the streets) whence they came, or where they went, or whether, when the lips moved, one kind word was said of him in all the year, than did the Chimes themselves.

What Christmas Is to a Bunch of People

Under the odd headline above, the Christmas 1851 issue of Household Words *picked up on the theme of Dickens' 'growing older' essay with pages of pen-pictures of various trades and professions. This is just a very small sample. It is no surprise to see the Beadle coming in for scornful treatment.*

What this period of the year is to THE GARDENER, we may easily guess, from great arms-full of mistletoe boughs, of holly-boughs thick with berries, and branches of laurel which he is continually carrying into the house, or going with as a present to neighbouring houses. And now, see him coming along with a bending back, bearing an entire fir-tree, which gracefully nods its head as he slowly trudges along, and shakes and rustles all its dry brown cones, as if in dumb anticipation of the peals of bells that will shortly be rung! This fir is for the Christmas Tree – the green and simple foundation and super-structure, which is shortly destined to sustain so much brightness and romance, so many glittering presents, and to be the medium of so many sweet feelings, joyous hopes, and tender sense of childhood – in present bright visions around us, and in tender recollections of the past.

* * *

As for THE NURSE, there can be no doubt but Christmas is a very anxious time for her. She expects so many of the young folks will make themselves very ill with all this quantity of plum-pudding, and plum-cake, and mince-pies. However, she consoles herself, on the whole, for any extra trouble she may have in pouring out, or mixing and stirring wine-glasses of physic, and trying to conceal powders in honey or red-currant jelly (and then getting them down!) by the proud recollection that she had the lady of the house in her arms when a child; and this consciousness makes her feel of the highest importance in the family.

* * *

If Christmas be a great fact to THE BEADLE, the Beadle seems a greater fact to Christmas. New broad-cloth – new scarlet and gold – new gold-laced cocked hat, of old Lord Mayor fashion – new gold-headed cane – no wonder that all the little charity boys eye his inflated presence with additional awe! No wonder that it is inflated; for he is swollen with the substantial comforts derived from all the great kitchens in the neighbourhood. There is a roasted ox in his mind. He can never forget the year when one was roasted whole upon the ice, and he present, and allowed to take his turn with the basting-ladle. It was the epic event of his life.

The Beadle is generally able to frown the charity boys into awe and silence; assisting the said frown, every now and then, with a few cuts of a long yellow twining cane, during service; whereby, amidst the sonorous tones of the preacher, there often breaks out a squealing cry from the hollow and remote aisles, or distant rows of heads in the organ loft, to the great injury of the eloquence of the pastor, and the gravity of the junior portion of his congregation.

But though this parish Terror of the Poor has portentous frowns for most of those under his dominion, he knows how to patronise with a smile, and his rubicund beams, at all seasons of festival, and more especially at Christmas, fall encouragingly upon all the cooks of the best houses round about. Perhaps, upon the chief Bell-ringer – perhaps, we may say, upon all the bell-ringers – and now and then upon the Sexton, with whom he does a little private business, in the way of gratuities from mourning relatives who come to visit graves. But as for the Pew-opener, envy of her gains at Christmas, and her obduracy in concealing their extent, renders him a foe to her existence, and haughtily unconscious of her presence as often as he can affect not to see her. There was, once upon a time, a good Beadle, who married a Pew-opener – but it was a long while ago – so long, that it is thought to have been in the good old . . . &c.

A Treat Denied

This clipping from the Bolton Chronicle *of 26 December 1857,
unearthed by Raymond Hargreaves for his book* Victorian Years,
Bolton 1850–60, *gives a first-hand account of the agonizing that went
on over the annual Christmas treat at the workhouse. Fortunately, there
is a happy ending, with private charity saving the day. All very
Victorian . . .*

The Chairman, in moving the resolution of which he gave notice last week, that the inmates of both workhouses be treated to roast beef and plum pudding as usual on Christmas Day, said that he was sorry there was to be so much opposition to it, as he had been told there would be.

Mr Cooper, the Assistant Clerk, had prepared a statement of the probable cost, with the proportion each township would have to contribute. From this it would appear that the total cost would be £21 3s 5d, of which some townships would have to contribute only 11d, and others who had no inmates in the workhouse, nothing. In the amount stated credit was not taken for food left, which would be used on the following day, thus reducing the amount by about £2, and if they made allowance also for the saving of the usual dinner, the actual cost would probably be reduced to £17. Mr Latham begged to move that the inmates of both workhouses have their usual Christmas treat.

Mr Alderman Dunderdale seconded the motion.

Mr Nuttall opposed it and thought that Great Bolton had already enough to do without incurring this extra expenditure. The Vice-Chairman moved that no such dinner or provision take place. He could never support the inmates of the workhouses being thus feasted while people outside were starving. It was really enough to send them to the workhouse.

Mr Taylor said he could not vote for the motion while there was so much distress outside. It was true it might only be a small trifle which some of the townships would have to contribute, but in the aggregate it would amount to a great sum.

Mr Brown supported the motion; it was only once a year they had the opportunity of giving these poor people a treat, and the poorest outside hardly ever passed over a year without a luxury of some sort.

The Vice-Chairman – Well, if they have it at their own expense let them have it.

Mr Brown continued – Those inside the workhouse had no luxuries. The Guardians had it in their power to give them a luxury once a year. Many children in the workhouse were orphans, it was their misfortune to be there. Many too were widows, and it was their misfortune to be there, and because it was their misfortune were they to

be deprived of that little Christmas cheer they had been accustomed to receive? He hoped not. They could let them have this treat now according to law, but not at any other time. Why then should they be so parsimonious as to refuse it, when it would cost so little?

Mr Brearley said he could not vote for the motion. He thought they should be just before they were generous out of the public purse. There were hundreds starving outside the workhouse who would be glad of beef and bread, let alone plum pudding, and if they did treat them he would rather the Guardians did it out of their own pocket and for that purpose he was willing to give £2. He was no advocate for eating and drinking out of the public purse.

Mr Skelton said he should be very glad if the poor people could have a treat but he was afraid that by giving them one the Guardians committed a very great mistake. He believed that on the day it was proposed to give the workhouse inmates these plum puddings, hundreds if not thousands of people in the Union would not have common and ordinary food.

Mr Hopwood said that he must say 'ditto' to almost all Mr Skelton had said. Mr Brown had gone too far when he laid so much stress upon the fatherless and widows.

Mr Brown – Fact.

Mr Hopwood – It is a fact likewise that three fourths of the people in the workhouse are rogues and vagabonds and only one fourth persons of good character.

Mr Hodson said that he could not let such an assertion pass unnoticed. The Governor told him that morning that there was not one able-bodied man in either establishment. He sympathised with the poor old creatures and also with the widows and orphans, and while he studied, as he ever did, the interests of the rate-payers, he would not deprive the poor people of the usual Christmas cheer. He trusted that no member of the Board would lack the spirit of humanity to deny it.

The Chairman said the bulk of them were old and infirm and then there were the children. He was an advocate of economy, but would bear his share of the responsibility in allowing the people this treat.

The question was then put, when the amendment was carried by 13 against 9.

Mr Hodson – I am sorry for that. The treat will, therefore, not be given.

The next week the Bolton Chronicle *carried the following:*

Captain Gray, one of Bolton's Members of Parliament, having heard of the Board's decision, had communicated to the Board his willingness to pay the full cost himself. The Board thereupon agreed that if the treat was to cost the Union nothing they could have it.

Rich Fare

These Christmas recipes come from the late Victorian magazine
The Woman at Home, *and what heavy fare they portray. Few writers of cookery columns today would think to end a recipe with the resounding phrase 'boiling curdles the blood'.*

Hare Soup

To make five pints of soup a fair-sized hare will be required. Cut it in small pieces, except the middle part of the back which should be kept whole. Take also one pound shin of beef, remove all fat and marrow from it; a quarter pound of lean ham, one pound of bones, two carrots, two large onions, a slice of turnip, four inches of celery, flavourings of marjoram, thyme and bay leaf, four cloves, ten pepper corns and a little salt. Put the head of the hare, the beef, bones, vegetables, and all the seasonings into a saucepan containing seven pints of cold water. When this boils, skim it carefully and put in the pieces of hare. Boil for three hours. It should be skimmed three times during the first hour. The middle cut of the back should be taken from the saucepan after being cooked for an hour and a half, and it can be made into an entrée or supper dish, as the soup will be quite rich enough without it. When the soup has boiled the full time strain it, pound or mince the meat from the hare; return it to the saucepan with the strained soup and three tablespoonfuls of flour mixed into a gill of ketchup and the same of port wine. Boil ten minutes to cook the flour thoroughly. Skim the soup once more. If the blood of the hare is added it must be done just before it is to be served, as boiling curdles the blood.

Mince Pies

Mincemeat must be made early in December, or it will not be fit for use at Christmas. It is often made without beef, but it is not so good if made merely of fruits and seasonings.

We give the ingredients required for three dozen small mince pies. One pound of large raisins, stone them and chop them small, a quarter of a pound of lean roast beef under-cooked, mince and pound it, half a pound of suet chopped as fine as to look like bread-crumb, one pound of sugar or a little more if liked sweet, four ounces of dates cut in small pieces, two large apples chopped fine, half a pound of mixed peel, which should be shredded, three ounces of pounded almonds, the juice of two lemons, a large grating of nutmeg, a pinch of ground cloves, a teaspoonful of cinnamon or allspice, a pinch of salt, a glass of brandy and two of sherry. After these ingredients have been well mixed, put them into a close fitting stone jar, press them very firmly, cover with paper dipped in whisky, and over the cover of the jar put a gummed paper, and in sixteen days the mincemeat will be ready for use.

Line the patty tins with good puff paste a quarter of an inch thick. Put

CHRISTMAS PUDDING.

When merry, frosty Christmas comes,
Mamma takes currants, peel, and plums;
Spice, raisins, flour, and eggs she takes,
And with them all a pudding makes;
So we are glad when Christmas comes
And brings us puddings full of plums.

a large spoonful of the mincemeat into each; cover with puff paste of the thickness before mentioned, and bake slowly for half an hour or forty minutes. The pies should be put into a brisk oven for the first ten minutes to raise the pastry, after that moderate the heat. When they are baked, brush them over with water and sprinkle castor sugar on them. Decorate the plates on which the mince pies are served with variegated holly.

Mince pies will keep good for two months if kept in a closed tin.

The Goblins Who Stole a Sexton

Charles Dickens

Dickens' love of the gothic and the grotesque is never better demonstrated than in the strange tale, an extract from which is printed here, recalled by the Wardles at Pickwick's Dingley Dell Christmas.

In an old abbey town, down in this part of the country, a long, long while ago – so long, that the story must be a true one, because our great-grandfathers implicitly believed it – there officiated as sexton and grave-digger in the churchyard, one Gabriel Grub. It by no means follows that because a man is a sexton, and constantly surrounded by emblems of mortality, therefore he should be a morose and melancholy man; your undertakers are the merriest fellows in the world; and I once had the honour of being on intimate terms with a mute, who in private life, and off duty, was as comical and jocose a little fellow as ever chirped out a devil-may-care song, without a hitch in his memory, or drained off the contents of a good stiff glass without stopping for breath. But, notwithstanding these precedents to the contrary, Gabriel Grub was an ill-conditioned, cross-grained, surly fellow – a morose and lonely man, who consorted with nobody but himself, and an old wicker bottle which fitted into his large deep waistcoat pocket – and who eyed each merry face, as it passed him by, with such a deep scowl of malice and ill-humour, as it was difficult to meet without feeling something the worse for.

A little before twilight, one Christmas-eve, Gabriel shouldered his spade, lighted his lantern, and betook himself towards the old churchyard; for he had got a grave to finish by next morning, and feeling very low, he thought it might raise his spirits, perhaps, if he went on with his work at once. As he went his way, up the ancient street, he saw the cheerful light of the blazing fires gleam through the old casements, and heard the loud laugh and the cheerful shouts of those who were assembled around them; he marked the bustling preparations for next day's cheer, and smelt the numerous savoury odours consequent thereupon, as they steamed up from the kitchen windows in clouds. All this was gall and wormwood to the heart of Gabriel Grub; and when groups of children bounded out of the houses, tripped across the road, and were met, before they could knock at the opposite door, by half-a-dozen curly-headed little rascals who crowded round them as they flocked up-stairs to spend the evening in their Christmas games, Gabriel smiled grimly, and clutched the handle of his spade with a firmer grasp as he thought of measles, scarlet fever, thrush, whooping-cough, and a good many other sources of consolation besides.

In this happy frame of mind, Gabriel strode along: returning a short, sullen growl to the good-humoured greetings of such of his neighbours as now and then passed him: until he turned into the dark lane which led to the churchyard. Now, Gabriel had been looking forward to reaching the dark lane because it was, generally speaking, a nice, gloomy, mournful place, into which the townspeople did not much care to go, except in broad daylight, and when the sun was shining; consequently, he was not a little

indignant to hear a young urchin roaring out some jolly song about a merry Christmas, in this very sanctuary, which had been called Coffin Lane ever since the days of the old abbey, and the time of the shaven-headed monks. As Gabriel walked on, and the voice drew nearer, he found it proceeded from a small boy, who was hurrying along, to join one of the little parties in the old street, and who, partly to keep himself company, and partly to prepare himself for the occasion, was shouting out the song at the highest pitch of his lungs. So Gabriel waited until the boy came up, and then dodged him into a corner, and rapped him over the head with his lantern five or six times, to teach him to modulate his voice. And as the boy hurried away with his hand to his head, singing quite a different sort of tune, Gabriel Grub chuckled very heartily to himself, and entered the churchyard: locking the gate behind him.

He took off his coat, put down his lantern, and getting into the unfinished grave, worked at it for an hour or so with right good will. But the earth was hardened with the frost, and it was no very easy matter to break it up, and shovel it out; and although there was a moon, it was a very young one, and shed little light upon the grave, which was in the shadow of the church. At any other time, these obstacles would have made Gabriel Grub very moody and miserable, but he was so well pleased with having stopped the small boy's singing, that he took little heed of the scanty progress he had made, and looked down into the grave, when he had finished work for the night, with grim satisfaction: murmuring as he gathered up his things:

> Brave lodgings for one, brave lodgings for one,
> A few feet of cold earth, when life is done;
> A stone at the head, a stone at the feet,
> A rich, juicy meal for the worms to eat;
> Rank grass overhead, and damp clay around,
> Brave lodgings for one, these, in holy ground!

'Ho! ho!' laughed Gabriel Grub, as he sat himself down on a flat tombstone, which was a favourite resting-place of his; and drew forth his wicker bottle. 'A coffin at Christmas! A Christmas Box. Ho! ho! ho!'

'Ho! ho! ho!' repeated a voice which sounded close behind him.

Gabriel paused in some alarm, in the act of raising the wicker bottle to his lips: and looked round. The bottom of the oldest grave about him was not more still and quiet than the churchyard in the pale moonlight. The cold hoar-frost glistened on the tombstones, and sparkled like rows of gems among the stone carvings of the old church. The snow lay hard and crisp upon the ground: and spread over the thickly-strewn mounds of earth so white and smooth a cover, that it seemed as if corpses lay there, hidden only by their winding-sheets. Not the faintest rustle broke the profound tranquillity of the solemn scene. Sound itself appeared to be frozen up, all was so cold and still.

'It was the echoes,' said Gabriel Grub, raising the bottle to his lips again.

'It was not,' said a deep voice.

Gabriel started up, and stood rooted to the spot with astonishment and terror; for his eyes rested on a form that made his blood run cold.

Seated on an upright tombstone, close to him, was a strange unearthly figure, whom Gabriel felt at once, was no being of this world. His long fantastic legs, which might have reached the ground, were cocked up, and crossed after a quaint, fantastic fashion; his sinewy arms were bare; and his hands rested on his knees. On his short round body, he wore a close covering, ornamented with small slashes; a short cloak dangled at his back; the collar was cut into curious peaks, which served the goblin in lieu of ruff or neckerchief; and his shoes curled up at the toes into long points. On his head he wore a broad-brimmed sugar-loaf hat, garnished with a single feather. The hat was covered with the white frost; and the goblin looked as if he had sat on the same tombstone very comfortably, for two or three hundred years. He was sitting perfectly still; his tongue was put out, as if in derision; and he was grinning at Gabriel Grub with such a grin as only a goblin could call up.

'It was not the echoes,' said the goblin.

Gabriel Grub was paralysed, and could make no reply.

'What do you do here on Christmas-eve?' said the goblin sternly.

'I came to dig a grave, sir,' stammered Gabriel Grub.

Christmas in the Navy

This Household Words *story from the middle of the last century is typical of the magazine's zeal in approaching Christmas from every angle.*

If there be any fire, above all fires, in which one ought to be able to see pleasant 'figures', it is a Christmas fire. So I will just plant myself opposite my log, and look for some pleasant images of memory, to recall Christmas at sea.

'Lash up hammocks!' The pipe of the boatswain's mate thrills shrilly through the lower-deck some winter morning, at four o'clock. You begin to be gradually aware that you are an officer in Her Majesty's service once more; that you belong to the 'Bustard'; and that you have got the morning watch. Of the last fact, the quartermaster makes you most thoroughly aware, by routing away at the 'nettles' of your hammock (very much like a boy routing out a blackbird's nest); and so does the young gentleman you are to relieve, who, having called the lieutenant of the next watch, glides alongside you, and says, 'Be quick up, Charley. I'm very sleepy.'

'Is it cold?'

'Infernally!'

You temporize for five minutes. You think about Lord Nelson. At last you hear 'Watch to muster!' You have to muster that watch. Out you jump, fling yourself into blanket trousers and a tremendous coat, and run up on deck. The watch are gathering aft; the quartermaster brings a lantern; you produce your watch-bill, and commence calling over the names. If you are a man of idle habits, your watch-bill is probably in an incorrect state. Among the main-top-men you come to the name 'Tomkins'. 'Tomkins!' you cry. No answer. 'Tomkins!' (with indignation). A voice answers 'Dead'. There is a kind of solemnity about that, which touches you rather poetically. But the lieutenant of your watch is affected by it in a more homely way, and indulges in a growl. However, a man's watch-bills, and quarter-bills, and division lists, can't be always right. I remember that my friend Childers, of the 'Rhinoceros', who had no division-list at all, used to bring up a copy of 'Thomson's Seasons', which looked rather like one, and by judiciously asking the men what their names were, first, and then roaring them out, afterwards, rubbed on very well.

You glance round the ship. The rigging is glittering with icicles, and looks like a tremendous chandelier. We suppose you to be at anchor somewhere. Halifax is a very good place for a winter scene – a very hospitable place, and capital quarters for salmon. Or, what do you say to Athens? It sounds too warm for a jolly Christmas; but, in reality, it is sometimes terribly cold. There is a wind that comes down from Russia as biting and peremptory as an ukase.

But at present we are in the 'Bustard'. She was a line-of-battle ship; and I will tell you, first, how they pass Christmas in a line-of-battle ship. The 'Bustard' was a credit to the profession; for she could sail right off at once, directly after she was launched, and was not repaired above twice in four years! We had a very pleasant Christmas in her, at anchor, in Vourla Bay, near the entrance of the Gulf of Smyrna. We had been looking after 'British interests' in Smyrna, that autumn, and had protected two balls, a masquerade, and several dinners at the consul's.

'It's getting near Christmas,' said the lieutenant of the watch to me after we had set the men to work holystoning, that morning.

'Very true, Sir,' I said, as if he had made a striking observation.

'Are you cold, Mr Topples?'

'Very, Sir,' I answered; for my 'Blue-veined feet unsandalled were', like Geraldine's, in 'Christabel'. They always made us keep the morning-watch barefoot in that precious 'Bustard'.

'Ah, you'd better walk about, then. Just lift that hammock-cloth over me,' said the lieutenant, composing himself in the nettings.

'Thank you.'

There was considerable discussion in the 'Bustard', how Christmas should be kept that year. Should the ward-room ask the gun-room and Captain to dinner? Or the Captain ask them? The last was impossible. Captain Barbell expected every man to do his duty – and to ask him. So we plucked up courage. We were an ambitious gun-room mess. One of that mess was a duke's son. It was notorious that we had Madeira, while the ward-room drank mere port. We invited the ward-room, and Captain Barbell. With a condescension which is the true charm of greatness, Captain Barbell accepted. I shall never forget my emotions when I saw him enter our mess-room, as if he had been a gentleman – (I mean, of course, as if he had been only an ordinary gentleman), and ask twice for soup!

It was a brilliant preparation that we had made to receive him. The tiller (which traverses the gun-room) was wrapped round with flag. The standards of every nation hung gracefully blended around in waves of colour. Eagles and trio-headed eagles swung together, as if they never pecked at each other – never laid bullets instead of jolly edible eggs – never fed on blood, or turned men into sausages! The mess looked like a menagerie. The British lion lay down with every conceivable animal. Friend Jonathan's stars helped the Turkish crescent to make a night of it; and the laurel which they all fight for (and which grows so impartially in every country) glittered tranquilly and green among them all.

But, before we went to dinner – just as the 'Roast Beef of Old England' was played, and Captain Barbell marched out of his cabin, looking very like the roast beef in question, raw – we all visited the lower deck where the seamen were beginning the evening. There, on the little tables, suspended by their polished bars, stood plum-puddings. Perhaps there were a couple to each mess – looking very like a pair of terrestrial and celestial globes. How the coppers ever hold these puddings, I mean some day to inquire, when I have found out who wrote 'Junius', why Ovid was banished from Rome, and some easier questions. These coppers had boiled a lake of cocoa that morning; had swallowed and boiled masses of junk, sparkling with lumps of salt; how they managed to hold the puddings, and to make them so good, I don't know, just now. Each pudding was decorated, perhaps with a paper ornament, perhaps with a sprig from some bush. Each 'great globe itself' vanished that night! I could feel no doubt of their destiny when I saw the expression

of the biggest fellow in the ship – the captain of the forecastle – as, like incense before the shrine of Neptune, his pudding sent up an awful steam before his weather-beaten face.

Old Christmas Day

Charles Rose

This recollection from a book of reminiscences of Dorking in Surrey, published in 1878, takes us back to the author's and Dickens' childhood in the days of George IV, when many elderly people still clung to the 'old' Christmas Day of the time before this country adopted the Gregorian calendar in 1752. In that year, 3 September became 14 September – but many Christian traditionalists could see no reason why this essentially secular piece of legislation should have any sway over what they were convinced was the true birth date of the Lord.

New Year's Day was celebrated in Dorking half a century ago much as it is at present. Then, as now, the departure of the old year and the coming in of the new were observed by different people in different ways.

The ringers rung the old year out and the new year in. Generally speaking, the ringing would commence but a short time before midnight, and continue only a brief period after. Sometimes, however, a thorough peal would be begun some hours before twelve, and would last till the new year had come.

These performances of the ringers were usually highly creditable, for Dorking at that time possessed a set of ringers equal at least to those of the neighbouring towns. The juniors who succeeded them attained, under the leadership of Mr Charles Boxall, a still greater proficiency.

Some in the olden period danced the old year out and the new year in, others thought it more becoming to spend the last moments of the old and the earliest of the new year in meditation and prayer; while of course the majority of the population passed the boundary line of time in unconscious repose. On the New Year's morning and throughout the day there were the same pleasant friendly greetings and hearty good wishes as there are now. New Year's gifts too were not forgotten.

Fifty years ago Old Christmas or Twelfth Day was more regarded than in the present day. There still lived then some of the sons and daughters of the venerable sires who saw the alteration of the Old Style, now within a year of a century-and-a-quarter ago. These worthy representatives of the olden time used to say of this change in the calendar that they never would believe that their parents went to bed one night and rose the next morning twelve days older than when they had sought their repose. Hence, like the Russians do in the present day, they adhered to the Old Style, thought little or nothing of New Christmas and pertinaciously kept the old day – and as they averred, the true one. On the last named, therefore, they regaled themselves and their households with Christmas fare, and those who had cattle reserved for them on that day the best corn and the best hay.

Christmas Was
a Little Late

This extract from Raymond Hargreaves' excellent Victorian Years, Bolton 1850–60 *serves as a reminder that before Christmas became one of the cornerstones of family life in the years of Victoria and Albert, it tended to be overlooked in many areas in favour of the more pagan joys of New Year. This is what the* Bolton Chronicle *had to say on the subject on 4 January 1851.*

Throughout Christendom Christmas is celebrated immediately it arrives, and the New Year no sooner dawns than it receives its homage. An exception to the rule, however, obtained in Bolton till within the last few years, which still partially remains. Not long ago the natal day of the Redeemer was pretty generally disregarded in this town, and a holiday was generally observed on New Year's Day. Now, though a holiday takes place on Christmas Day, the beginning of the New Year is looked upon as the Christmas season, and the inhabitants betake themselves to their festivities accordingly. Christmas geese, pies, puddings and beer don't see the light until New Year's Eve, and Christmas weddings and parties are deferred till the following day.

This was the order of things in regard to the past festive season.

Christmas Day having passed with its cessation from labour and its appointed ordinances, New Year's Eve overtook us on Tuesday, at the close of which day the mills, foundries, bleaching establishments, etc. were closed, some for the day, others for two, and the work people retired to their homes in anticipation of an annual treat.

The termination at midnight of 1850 was speedily followed by the ringing of bells of the Parish Church and for hours before the break of day sounds of music were plentifully poured forth in the streets by companies of vocalists and instrumentalists, indicative of the compliments of the season. The fall of a considerable quantity of rain seemed not to damp the ardour of persons going about to wish their friends a happy New Year.

The weather at this festive time was quite of an unusual character, frost and snow being out of the question, and the atmosphere exceedingly mild. On New Year's Day from nine o'clock till four, little, if any, rain descended. The town rapidly became a scene of life and bustle, and so it continued until evening approached. Boys and girls, young men and maids, fathers and mothers, thronged the streets in quest of pleasure. The 'festive array' in which many of the Boltonians and their visitors were clad bore ample testimony to the existence of that 'prosperity' which everyone desired to reign throughout the year, and the very 'respectable' nature of the apparel displayed on the backs of the working classes strikingly illustrated the cheapness and plenitude of articles of dress. Candidates for married bliss were moderately prominent in processions, wending their way amidst the 'busy hum of men'. Bands of music passed stylishly through the borough, and added an air of 'harmony' to that of goodwill. The multitudes of country people who flocked to the town in the early part of the day increased the population vastly above its ordinary amount, and the 'fair' was attended most numerously.

The principal streets were crowded to an extent which was rarely, if ever, exceeded. The shops were set out to the best advantage. Stalls with oranges, nuts, gingerbread and other eatable nicnacs, which it would be wearisome to enumerate, were abundant, and there was no lack of toys either in regard to quantity or variety. On the market place holiday amusements in the shape of swinging-boats, whirligigs, etc were in active operation, and there was an abundance of shows and showmen, professing to enlighten, inform or amuse on subjects natural and unnatural, historical and dramatical, artistical, mystical, gymnastical. On no former occasion in our remembrance has the market place been so densely crowded as it was on Wednesday by pleasure seekers, money seekers and their appliances. Not the least remarkable sight in the town generally was the great number of those who had imbibed to an immoderate extent the infusions of malt and other potent beverages. In the evening, Sunday school and Congregational tea parties were held in different parts of the town, and other means of recreation were resorted to.

Sir Joseph's Great Dinner

Charles Dickens

Bowley and Cute – the great villains of The Chimes *– are here living it up on New Year's Day at Bowley Hall, until unwelcome news and their reaction to it allow Dickens to let rip at the boss class's hypocrisy.*

Sir Joseph Bowley, Friend and Father of the Poor, held a great festivity at Bowley Hall, in honour of the natal day of Lady Bowley; and as Lady Bowley had been born on New Year's Day (which the local newspapers considered an especial pointing of the finger of Providence to number One, as Lady Bowley's destined figure in Creation), it was on a New Year's Day that this festivity took place.

Bowley Hall was full of visitors. The red-faced gentleman was there, Mr Filer was there, the great Alderman Cute was there – Alderman Cute had a sympathetic feeling with great people, and had considerably improved

his acquaintance with Sir Joseph Bowley on the strength of his attentive letter: indeed had become quite a friend of the family since then – and many guests were there. Trotty's ghost was there, wandering about, poor phantom, drearily; and looking for its guide.

There was to be a great dinner in the Great Hall. At which Sir Joseph Bowley, in his celebrated character of Friend and Father of the Poor, was to make his great speech. Certain plum-puddings were to be eaten by his Friends and Children in another Hall first; and, at a given signal, Friends and Children flocking in among their Friends and Fathers, were to form a family assemblage, with not one manly eye therein unmoistened by emotion.

But there was more than this to happen. Even more than this. Sir Joseph Bowley, Baronet and Member of Parliament, was to play a match at skittles – real skittles – with his tenants.

'Which quite reminds one,' said Alderman Cute, 'of the days of old King Hal, stout King Hal, bluff King Hal. Ah, fine character!'

'Very,' said Mr Filer, dryly. 'For marrying women and murdering 'em. Considerably more than the average number of wives by the bye.'

'You'll marry the beautiful ladies, and not murder 'em, eh?' said Alderman Cute to the heir of Bowley, aged twelve. 'Sweet boy! We shall have this little gentleman in Parliament now,' said the Alderman, holding him by the shoulders, and looking as reflective as he could, 'before we know where we are. We shall hear of his successes at the poll; his speeches in the House; his overtures from Governments; his brilliant achievements of all kinds; ah! we shall make our little orations about him in the Common Council, I'll be bound; before we have time to look about us!'

'Oh, the difference of shoes and stockings!' Trotty thought. But his heart yearned towards the child, for the love of those same shoeless and stockingless boys, predestined (by the Alderman) to turn out bad, who might have been the children of Meg.

* * *

'Bless my heart and soul!' cried Mr Fish. 'Where's Alderman Cute? Has anybody seen the Alderman?'

Seen the Alderman? Oh dear! Who could ever help seeing the Alderman? He was so considerate, so affable; he bore so much in mind the natural desire of folks to see him; that if he had a fault, it was the being constantly On View. And wherever the great people were, there, to be sure, attracted by the kindred sympathy between great souls, was Cute.

Several voices cried that he was in the circle round Sir Joseph. Mr Fish made his way there; found him; and took him secretly into a window near at hand. Trotty joined them. Not of his own accord. He felt that his steps were led in that direction.

'My dear Alderman Cute,' said Mr Fish. 'A little more this way. The most dreadful circumstance has occurred. I have this moment received the intelligence. I think it will be best not to acquaint Sir Joseph with it till the day is over. You understand Sir Joseph, and will give me your opinion. The most frightful and deplorable event!'

'Fish!' returned the Alderman. 'Fish! My good fellow, what is the matter? Nothing revolutionary, I hope! No – no attempted interference with the magistrates?'

'Deedles, the banker,' gasped the Secretary. 'Deedles Brothers – who was to have been here to-day – high office in the Goldsmiths' Company –'

'Not stopped!' exclaimed the Alderman. 'It can't be!'

'Shot himself.'

'Good God!'

'Put a double-barrelled pistol to his mouth, in his counting-house,' said Mr Fish, 'and blew his brains out. No motive. Princely circumstances!'

'Circumstances!' exclaimed the Alderman. 'A man of noble fortune. One of the most respectable of men. Suicide, Mr Fish! By his own hand!'

'This very morning,' returned Mr Fish.

'Oh the brain, the brain!' exclaimed the pious Alderman, lifting up his hands. 'Oh the nerves, the nerves; the mysteries of this machine called Man! Oh the little that unhinges it: poor creatures that we are! Perhaps a dinner, Mr Fish. Perhaps the conduct of his son, who, I have heard, ran very wild, and was in the habit of drawing bills upon him without the least authority! A most respectable man! But there is One above. We must submit, Mr Fish. We must submit!'

What, Alderman! No word of Putting Down? Remember, Justice, your high moral boast and pride. Come, Alderman! Balance those scales. Throw me into this, the empty one. No Dinner, and Nature's founts in some poor woman, dried by starving misery and rendered obdurate to claims for which her offspring has authority in holy mother Eve. Weigh me the two, you Daniel going to judgment, when your day shall come! Weigh them, in the eyes of suffering thousands, audience (not unmindful) of the grim farce you play! Or supposing that you strayed from your five